RICHARD HADLEE: AT THE DOUBLE

RICHARD HADLEE:

At the Double

The Story of Cricket's Pacemaker

Richard Hadlee
with Tony Francis

STANLEY PAUL
London Melbourne Sydney Auckland Johannesburg

Stanley Paul & Co. Ltd.

An imprint of the Hutchinson Publishing Group

17-21 Conway Street, London W1P 6JD

Hutchinson Publishing Group (Australia) Pty. Ltd.
16-22 Church Street, Hawthorn, Melbourne, Victoria 3122
89-91 Albion Street, Surrey Hills, Sydney, N.S.W. 2010

Hutchinson Group (N.Z.) Ltd.
32-34 View Road, P.O. Box 40-086, Glenfield, Auckland, 10

Hutchinson Group (S.A.) Pty. Ltd.
P.O. Box 337, Bergvlei 2012, South Africa

First published 1985
© Richard Hadlee and Tony Francis 1985

Set in 12/13 pt Times
Printed and bound in New Zealand by
Whitcoulls Ltd., Christchurch

ISBN 0 09 160870 8

Contents

Acknowledgements

I should like to thank Peter Wynne-Thomas, the Notts statistician for his painstaking assistance (good luck with your anthology). Thanks also to John Sumpter and Adrian Murrell for the photographs; to Clive Rice, Ken Taylor and Fred Titmus for their wisdom, and, not least, to my wife Shelley for her time at the transcription desk.

The Author

Tony Francis is Central Television's sports presenter. He achieved his own 'double' in 1984 — completing the 100-year history of Derby County Football Club, *There Was Some Football Too*, and writing this insight into one of the most unusual cricketers of our times.

The author has travelled the world covering cricket tours, Olympic Games and World Cup football for ITV.

He had the honour of bowling a maiden over to Richard Hadlee during a testimonial match last summer. Not everyone can say that!

Tony is a modern languages graduate from St John's College, Cambridge and lives in Nottingham with his wife and three sons.

Introduction

I was enjoying a lager with Richard Hadlee at Central Television's Nottingham studios when he remarked, in that casual way of his, that he was hoping to achieve the 'double'. Considering that the summer was barely into its stride, it seemed a singularly ambitious statement. The more I listened, the more fascinated I became. Was he seriously 'planning' to equal Fred Titmus's achievement of seventeen years earlier? How do you *PLAN* it?

Richard's logic was faultless and his sharply-focused vision of the coming months quite disconcerting.

As the conversation progressed, I had the feeling that I could be talking to a robot. Richard seemed to be programmed from without. There had to be an explanation, and there was.

He told me about his mental breakdown in November 1983 and subsequent recovery. The transformation owed everything, it emerged, to a fast-talking guru he met quite by chance in New Zealand. Some discover faith. Richard had discovered the power of positive thought. Now read on . . .

Tony Francis

1

Double Vision

Well before the South African Airways Boeing 747 touched down at Heathrow, Richard Hadlee had decided that 1984 would be his season. Yes, DECIDED! When he gets an idea into his head, there's no shifting it.

With Hadlee on that flight from Johannesburg were his wife, Karen and young son, Nicholas. The family had been enjoying a few days break at the home of Nottinghamshire's South African captain, Clive Rice, before chasing the summer again. The routine was a familiar one by now. Twice a year they packed their belongings for the two-day journey from one corner of the globe to the opposite. This was always the painful leg, leaving their home in Christchurch and saying goodbye to relations and friends for the next five months or so.

That historic series victory over England had hardly been celebrated and the 'unknown' tour of Sri Lanka successfully negotiated than it was time to head back 14,000 miles to Hadlee's second home, Nottingham.

Looking out through the brilliant April sunshine over England's distinctive patchwork of green and yellow, Hadlee first had the feeling that the gods were on his side. If this weather held, his task would be that much easier. Funny how things work out. He had topped the first-class bowling averages for the last three seasons, yet in the autumn of 1980 he had been ready to quit English cricket for good. Hadlee's mind drifted back to that moment four years ago when everything seemed to be falling apart.

I stood on the players' balcony at Trent Bridge waving farewell to the supporters and firmly believing that I'd played my last game for Nottinghamshire. It was a highly charged occasion. My mum and dad were there, and alongside me on the balcony were Clive Rice and those legendary England pace bowlers from the Bodyline tour, Bill Voce and Harold Larwood. I don't mind telling you I felt a lump in my throat. But standing in that company I felt a cheat. I had had three awful seasons since first joining the club in 1978. Injuries and commitments to New Zealand meant that I hadn't given Notts value for money. I was embarrassed to collect my pay cheque. That 1980 season seemed like the final straw. I managed only seven out of twenty-two championship matches because of injury and decided I'd best be on my way.

Curiously, Hadlee 'signed off' in the most dramatic fashion, taking a career-best 6—12 in the closing Sunday League game against Lancashire. The shortened run-up, favoured by most pacemen on Sundays, had proved more devastating than he imagined. It was to be the key to the future, though, of course, Hadlee didn't realise it at the time. Fans, team mates and committee members conspired to keep him at Trent Bridge.

Within a few hours of that balcony send-off, the club chairman, John Heatley called Hadlee into his office and asked him to come back next season, even if he bowled off two paces. The same message was echoed around the dressing room. Rice also pointed out that he could earn as much in five months as he could in a full year in New Zealand.

What could I say? The club, the players and the supporters had given me a tremendous vote of confidence. I had to come back for another go. It was at that moment that I decided to use the Sunday run-up at all times. I figured it would relieve the wear and tear on my body and increase my life in cricket.

What he couldn't foresee was the flak he would take back home in New Zealand. The crowds wouldn't accept Hadlee operating off a fifteen metre approach instead of his usual twenty metres. They didn't seem to take into account that he was now in his thirtieth year. It takes an extraordinary man to bowl 'consistently fast in modern day cricket without breaking down. The demands of Test series and one-day competitions, not to mention the domestic seasons have taken their toll on most of the world's greats . . . Dennis Lillee, Bob Willis, Michael Holding, Imran Khan, etc. Hadlee was bitterly upset at the reaction down under.

Their failure to accept my short run was one of the biggest disappointments I've had. Injuries were coming far too frequently bowling fast ten months of the year. I suffered from a sore left ankle which still worries me today and appears to be a joint problem which is unlikely to improve. I found it much easier on my ankle to bowl off the shorter approach because there was far less pressure placed on it.

What I wanted was to relinquish my role as my country's number one shock bowler. Bowling off the short run makes life far more enjoyable and it would have suited me fine to drop into the first change role if a couple of young quickies came along to relieve me. My outstanding season with Notts in the championship year of 1981 made me realise that my effectiveness was much greater off the limited run-up. I took 105 wickets and topped the English averages with 14.89. I could bowl for longer periods, and do more with the ball. What I sacrificed in pace, I more than made up for in variation. The number of victims was there to prove it. The bouncer and the quicker ball were always up my sleeve, so the surprise element was more effective.

When I arrived in New Zealand, I used the short run for my provincial side, Canterbury, and it was just as successful. It was one of my best seasons, 59 wickets at fewer than fifteen runs apiece. In the Second Test against the Australians at Eden Park in the 1981-82 series, I bowled off a short run in the first innings, took 2 – 38 off twenty overs and felt that I'd done a good job. The crowd didn't agree. 'Who's the new spin bowler?' they asked. People wouldn't accept my professional judgement.

The New Zealand captain, Geoff Howarth wanted me to go back to the long run, especially with the new ball, but

11

I was adamant. It was only under the severest pressure and out of frustration at what the 'knockers' were saying that I reverted to the long run in the second innings. As it happened, I took five wickets which seemed to prove the detractors right.

The media gave me such a hard time on the first day that I was almost in tears by the end of it. Not like me at all. It was pressure I didn't need. One local reporter, Don Cameron, described me this way: 'New Zealand's heaviest artillery operating off a pop-gun run-up.' I was accused of firing corks. That really hurt. I was so upset, I even thought of telling the selectors I wouldn't be available for the last Test! I thought better of it.

Hadlee had returned to Notts for the 1981 season with limited ambitions. If he could get through most of the season without injury, everyone would be happy. As we know, the season ended with Notts celebrating their first championship title in fifty-two years. Committee men were weeping with the sheer emotion of it all, not least Reg Simpson, the former Notts and England batsman who'd never experienced anything like it.

To everyone's amazement, and probably my own, I got through all the championship games and only missed one Sunday League match when I was rested against Warwickshire. When we won the championship, we took the salute from the Trent Bridge balcony . . . the same balcony from which I'd been waving goodbye only twelve months earlier. Astonishing. In the four years that I'd been at Notts we'd finished 17th, 13th, 3rd, and then 1st.

There was, and still is, a fair amount of criticism of the Trent Bridge wicket. Ron Allsop, the groundsman had been instructed, along with all groundsmen, to prepare wickets for positive cricket. He did that alright. In the ten games played there that season, there were nine results. We won eight and lost one. Yet the media criticised him for 'cheating' because he allegedly 'doctored' wickets for Clive Rice and myself. That was nonsense. Our off-spinner, Eddie Hemmings collected 50 of his 90 wickets at Trent Bridge! The truth was that the opposition let themselves be psyched out. They got it into their heads that they couldn't score runs on our wickets, and played like novices. They just gave up.

In any case, Notts wasn't the only club with fast bowling strength, so why didn't others exploit the conditions like we did? What was obvious was that when we played away, many pitches were low and slow to nullify Clive's and my own effectiveness. If that's not cheating, I don't know what is. The pitch at Chelmsford was prepared for the Essex spinners, Acfield and East, and Hove was always hard and fast for Le Roux and Imran. The majority of my wickets were taken at Trent Bridge but 45 were captured away from home. Some of my best performances were on unresponsive tracks. I took 7−25 at Liverpool, 6−61 at Chelmsford and 4−19 at Bradford. That gave me a great deal of pleasure because the wickets had been doctored to blunt me.

The same sort of thing was happening in 1984 when we came agonisingly close to winning our second championship. Once again, poor old Ron Allsop was reported when he should have been congratulated for achieving exactly what the Test and County Cricket Board wanted, results.

In the title-winning season of 1981, Hadlee finished with 745 runs as well as those 105 wickets. Yet it had never occurred to him to attempt the English double of 1,000 runs and 100 wickets in a season. Until that year his wicket hauls had been in the 70's and 80's. It wasn't until about three quarters of the way through 1981 that Ken Taylor, the Notts manager, pointed out to him the possibility of the double. 'What do you mean?' asked Hadlee, 'what double?' When it was explained he looked at the statistics.

I worked out that it was just about possible, but we had only seven games left and most of them were won in two days. It meant that I didn't get a second innings, so with one or two failures with the bat as well, the chance was gone. I still finished only 255 runs short and felt that I'd been robbed by the circumstances.

The following season, 1982, was an even bigger disappointment, both for Notts and Hadlee. Rice and the newly-recruited Mike Hendrick both suffered badly with injuries and though Hadlee raced to 49 wickets in the first half of the season, he succumbed to a hamstring strain and made only brief bowling appearances for the rest of the summer. Coming in off no more than five paces, he collected another 13 wickets and still ended up top of the championship bowling averages for the third successive season. Any thoughts of the double had been torpedoed, though Hadlee began to discover that he was a better batsman than he'd given himself credit for.

Notts moved him up the order to number six and he repaid them with 807 runs at an average of 31. The hamstring didn't restrict him. Scores of 131 against Surrey and 98 against Gloucestershire are testimony to that. What's more, batting at number three, he made 100 not out also against Gloucestershire in a Sunday League match. There was no doubt that Hadlee's batting was improving with every season.

With it came the growing realisation that the double ought to be within his grasp. Hadlee did some research and discovered that no cricketer in modern times had achieved it. The Middlesex and England all-rounder, Fred Titmus was the last one to reach the target in 1967. That was before the domestic game was slimmed down, in 1969. Before then, it was a relatively comfortable target for an all-rounder. In the 1920's Frank Woolley took 100 wickets and scored 2,000 runs in three consecutive seasons. In 1921 and 1922 he came within thirty-odd wickets of equalling G. H. Hirst's all-time record of 200 wickets and 2,000 runs, set in 1906.

Also in the 1920's, Maurice Tate scored 1,000 runs and claimed 200 wickets in three successive summers. Since the war, Trevor Bailey is the only cricketer to achieve the 2,000 runs and 100 wickets milestone. That was in 1959. Bailey, along with Titmus and others did the standard 1,000 runs and 100 wickets double on eight occasions. Wilfred Rhodes did it sixteen times, Hirst, fourteen.

After 1969, when the number of county games was reduced, only five players have managed to score 1,000 runs and take 75 wickets in a season. They are Mushtaq Mohammad (1969), Tony Greig (1971), Richard Hutton (1971), Keith Boyce (1972) and Mike Procter (1979).

14

The more Hadlee looked into it, the more he fancied the challenge. He was running out of time. The 1983 summer was a write-off because of the New Zealand tour of England. He made up his mind:

It had to be 1984. I was getting older and the years left at Trent Bridge were becoming fewer and fewer. I sat down and planned how I would do the double that summer.

2

The Budget

In the nicest sense of the expression, Hadlee is a computerised cricketer — a scientist who works out his method and conclusion and leaves nothing to chance. His bowling style captures the essence of the man; efficient, economical and arguably the most consistent in the world. He talks and behaves in much the same manner. Those who don't know or understand him can mistake it for arrogance or rudeness. It is neither. He is admittedly intolerant of wastefulness or lack of professionalism. That can often make him a difficult person to live and play cricket with, but that's the price he pays.

The double was not a misty romantic notion — more like a military exercise, to be planned and executed with cold-blooded precision. There were 100 victims to be gunned down and 1,000 runs to be carved out. He thought he knew precisely where and how it was to be done. Hadlee wrote out his budget for the season and we shall see how uncannily accurate it was. Why go to so much trouble?

I have played first-class cricket for fourteen years and enjoyed tremendous success. I've played in more Test match victories than any other New Zealander and have been in championship winning teams. But in recent years, motivation has been very difficult. The only things that really keep me going are statistics and reaching targets. It got to the stage where cricket was becoming a bore so I needed a new challenge every season. Doing the double was the most detailed plan of attack I've ever undertaken. There were so many things that could have gone wrong—injury, the weather, the state of the game—all of them could deny me. The fact that I ended up playing more games than I budgeted for was a real bonus. For a start, it was a marvellous summer. We only missed two and a half days through rain.

I remained pretty free from injury though there was a time when I picked up a virus in the key Natwest trophy match against Middlesex. I was bowling off three or four paces because my legs wouldn't carry me. I had no energy. It was in July, just after my thirty-third birthday and I felt my age that day I can tell you.

We were expected to win the game but disappointed our supporters at Trent Bridge by batting badly after dismissing Middlesex for 228 in 59.5 overs. I took 2−33 in my twelve overs but I was exhausted at the end of it. It was probably a combination of doing more batting and bowling than usual, of the extra strain of trying to stay around the top of the championship table while Essex and Leicestershire were going well, and of aiming for my personal target. Anyway, Notts could only manage 223 runs in reply and we were out of the competition. Apart from that day, however, I felt good all season.

Unlike in Titmus's day, we didn't have twenty-eight games to play. The figure was twenty-four and I worked out that with a reasonable summer, we might get through twenty of those. The simple calculation was that I needed five wickets and 50 runs a game. It never happens that way of course. A couple of failures with the bat, or a few innings victories and you could be left high and dry. I had to look at the thing in more detail.

I said to myself that to get 100 wickets, I had to get 60 of them at Trent Bridge. That was going to be my best chance. It left me with 40 victims to account for away from Trent Bridge. With the runs, it was exactly the opposite, 400 at Nottingham and 600 away from home. Another way of looking at it was that for every wicket I took, I had to score ten runs with the bat. I tried all sorts of formulae.

To get the 100 wickets, I decided I needed 10 bags of five, and I could virtually nominate the grounds or the opposition where I had my best chance. Lancashire is one that sticks out in my mind. I've also had successes over the years against Surrey, Leicestershire, Yorkshire, Essex, Derbyshire, Gloucestershire and Sussex. I've never done very much against Warwickshire, Hampshire or Glamorgan and Somerset I've only faced once or twice in my seven years at Trent Bridge.

Hadlee religiously wrote down his twelve targets for the season. He kept the list in a folder in his cricket bag:

1. *First bowler to reach 100 wickets.*
2. *Better career-best first-class bowling record of 7—23 (against India in 1975-76 and Sussex at Trent Bridge in 1979).*
3. *Ten bags of five wickets.*
4. *Sixty wickets at Trent Bridge, forty away.*
5. *Better career-best batting (142 not out against Yorkshire at Bradford in 1981).*
6. *Six hundred runs away from home and four hundred at Trent Bridge.*
7. *Three centuries and six fifties.*
8. *The double.*
9. *Player of the Year.*
10. *All-rounder of the Year.*
11. *I must help win ten matches in the championship with an inspired individual performance.*
12. *Take 25 catches.*

As it turned out, the evergreen John Lever of Essex beat Hadlee to the 100 wickets. He failed to better his best bowling performance, 7—35 against Gloucestershire was his outstanding effort of the summer. On the batting side, he spectacularly surpassed his 142 not out at Bradford in the 1981 title-winning season by scoring an unbeaten 210 against Middlesex at Lords towards the end of the season. Hadlee also exceeded his expectations by scoring 711 runs away from home and 468 at Trent Bridge.

While only collecting five wickets on three occasions, he had two hauls of six, one of seven, but more importantly, eleven bags of four. Of his total of 117 wickets, 74 were collected at Trent Bridge and 43 away. Once again, in line with his plan but exceeding his budget. As for the three centuries and six fifties, well, he DID score six fifties and made up for the centuries with that 210 at Middlesex and 100 not out against Hampshire at Bournemouth.

On top of all that, I badly wanted to be voted Player of the Year, which I was, and All-rounder of the Year, which I was. I felt I had to help win ten matches during the season with an inspired individual performance. In other words, if there could have been a man of the match award each game, I wanted to win it ten times at least. In short, I wanted everything that season, the lot.

That was not the end of Hadlee's budget. He was even more scientific.

He budgeted 20 championship matches and played 24.
He budgeted 31 innings and played 33.
The target was 1,000 runs. He scored 1179.
He budgeted for a batting average of 34. It was 51.2.
For the bowling, he estimated 750 overs and bowled 772.
He budgeted on 250 maidens and bowled 248.
He planned to give away 1500 runs and gave away 1645.
The 100 wicket target turned out to be 117.
His bowling average was estimated at 15. It turned out to be 14.05.

Hadlee extended his budget to cover the John Player League and the two cup competitions, the Benson and Hedges and the Natwest Trophy. If you pressed him, he'd probably tell you where he'd be and what he'd be doing on any given day of the coming year! It's an attitude and approach to the game that would be foreign to most cricketers, and might almost qualify him for residence at number 11 Downing Street! Can you, for instance imagine Hadlee's great rival, Ian Botham setting out his stall in such meticulous fashion?

The nearest thing to Hadlee in that sense is probably Geoff Boycott. He too appears to be driven by the desire to gather records and thereby chisel himself a slice of immortality. Both men could 'score' a match as well as play in it. Boycott admits that he rarely needs the luxury of a scoreboard when he's grinding out another long innings — he knows exactly how many runs he has to his name. On at least one occasion he's corrected a scorer who devalued his contribution! Hadlee is made of the same stuff.

He admits that his driving ambition is fuelled by insecurity and lack of confidence. On the face of it, an unusual admission from one of the world's outstanding cricketers, but understandable if one takes the time to consider. To begin with, his nationality is against him. Being a New Zealander until recent times was like playing soccer for Hartlepools.

Having a great cricket nation like Australia on the doorstep didn't make it any easier. It wasn't until the 1973-74 series that Australia agreed to play official Test matches on a regular basis against New Zealand. Even now, with a series victory against England and the West Indies behind them, the memories of those humble origins still linger.

There's no question that being a New Zealander was a bad start in a cricketing sense. We all lacked confidence at birth I guess. We could see the tough way the Australians played the game and longed to be able to do that, to give them a battle. We were the nice guys. Other countries would rub their hands when they they played the Kiwis, it meant players could increase their batting aggregates and bowling tallies. Rather like Sri Lanka today, we were considered cannon fodder (though David Gower might blush at that!). We were expected to lose every match, even by our most ardent supporters. If we drew, we'd done well, if we actually won a game, unbelievable! We'd declare a national holiday.

It was exactly the opposite with the All Blacks . . and that made things worse. If the rugby team lost it was DISASTER. Thank goodness, it's all changing now. We were the last team to beat the mighty West Indians and no-one can take us for granted. We've gradually grown to be more professional. It was a great advantage to have our guys playing in England. Glenn Turner was the first, followed by Geoff Howarth, John Parker, myself, John Wright, and now Martin Crowe at

Somerset. We have learned a lot to pass onto the younger players and harden their approach to the game. The results have been incredible in the last four to five years. There's been a revolution in our cricket.

The way I've played in that time, especially in England, it's as though I've something to prove. I want to go out there and show that I can get wickets, score runs and help win matches. Not just now and then, but every day! I suppose I'm proving it to myself as well as to others, and I'm sure it all comes back to that fundamental lack of confidence because I'm a New Zealander.

There's no way that I would ever put my own personal performance ahead of the team. I'd never play for my average. Although achieving the 'double' came to mean so much to me, I would have sacrificed it for the sake of the team if the circumstances had demanded. It may look from the way I planned it all that I'm a selfish cricketer and I'm certain there are those who believe it to be so. The reason I did it was to put pressure on myself to reach a difficult target, and, hopefully, to help some of the younger members of the club to learn about application, determination and professionalism.

What Hadlee's colleagues did not realise was that his brilliant career had almost come to a shuddering halt only five months before he set out on his 'double' mission. Not because of physical injury this time. It was more serious than that.

3

Mental Breakdown

The Hadlee family has become the royal line in New Zealand cricket. First Walter, captain of the 1949 touring team to England, manager of the 1965 side, and closely associated ever since. Then Dayle and Barry who didn't quite manage to scale the heights. And now Richard, arguably the best cricketer the two islands have ever produced. Living up to the family tradition created pressure as a youngster — living with it created problems of a different sort now.

Being a national hero can be tough. It means you are public property and, like it or not, you have to go along with that. Whereas a writer or a musician for example can escape to the shadows in his private life knowing that once his reputation is made, his future is secure, a sportsman has no such security. His time at the top is limited, however good he may be. From the age of thirty when other professionals are perhaps building up to peak prosperity, the sportsman knows that his physical capabilities are starting to wane and that his earning potential wanes with it.

For that reason, he has to capitalize on the good times while they last. That means propelling himself into the public gaze at every opportunity, saying 'yes' to every lucrative spin-off. Time to socialize, time to spend with the family, and time to sit back and relax is at a premium.

So it was with Hadlee when he returned to New Zealand after the 1983 tour of England. New Zealand had lost the series, but achieved their first victory on English soil.

Reaction to it back home was phenomenal. New Zealand cricket had arrived at long last. Television viewers and radio listeners had witnessed the scenes at Headingley for themselves, so it doesn't take much imagination to capture the joyous welcome-home the players received.

Hadlee had been in demand for years, but those demands became enormous now—'frightening' to use his word. Some of the pressure was self-inflicted.

There's no security for a professional sportsman or woman. All cricketers who perform in England are on a one to three year contract and there's always a danger it might not be renewed. If it isn't, the player somehow has to find a new job, and they're not easy to come by. Consequently, there's tremendous pressure to perform consistently well to earn your crust of bread. When you are doing well, the money's good, but it can all be over so quickly. A bad injury can wipe out everything overnight.

Hadlee does considerably more than play cricket for a living. He has his own promotion company, is a publicity officer for Leopard Breweries in New Zealand, promotes Adidas sportswear, prepares a weekly cricket programme for the local radio station 3ZB, writes newspaper and magazine columns, makes television commercials and is highly sought-after as a guest speaker. His agent is Mark McCormack. He's written four books himself, and plans to write more. That New Zealand spring (or English autumn) of 1983, his diary hardly allowed him time to draw breath!

There were deadlines to meet—more than I can ever recall before. The after-dinner speaking engagements had piled up. It might surprise some people to know that speaking in public doesn't come easily. I'm expected to amuse, entertain and instruct—very nerve-wracking. Twenty minutes of it and I'm drained. When I came back from England, the promotional work was heavier than ever as well. Every day it seemed there were people to meet and functions to open. I was trying to reach a deadline on my latest book while dashing around speaking at school assemblies all over the country.

I was literally flying to work. I would fly off to Auckland

for half a day, then hundreds of miles to Wellington in the afternoon before flying back to Christchurch in the evening for another appointment and falling into bed at some unearthly hour of the night. On top of that, I had responsibilities to the New Zealand Cricket Council coaching committee which required me to do at least three weeks of fast bowling tuition. Something had to give.

Hadlee was on his way to a mental and physical breakdown. It may have been precipitated by a virus infection he contracted in Wellington in November. On the other hand, he could have collected the virus simply because his body was so run-down. For a few weeks he'd been feeling under the weather, but he continued his punishing routine of engagements until he came to a dead stop.

I was playing in a festival match at Rotorua — New Zealand against an invitation team which included Mike Gatting, Norman Cowans and Derek Underwood. I started the game but couldn't go on. I came off the pitch in a daze, wondering what the hell was happening to me. I couldn't see properly and my head was splitting. Somehow I got home and went to bed.

Over the following few days I seemed to have lost the will to do anything. At home I became terribly neurotic. I'm a fastidious person at the best of times, but it got to the stage where every tiny problem was magnified out of proportion. If a picture on the wall wasn't straight, I had to straighten it; if there was a smudge mark on the window, I had to get up and clean it. It was the same with my cricket trophies — I was constantly polishing them. It was ridiculous. Even a dead fly on the floor had to be picked up or I couldn't relax!

After a few weeks of this, I snapped completely. Everything was too much for me. The thought of another cricket season around the corner and a Test series against England just about finished me off. Looking back, I can see that I was undergoing a mental and physical collapse, although I didn't realise it at the time. I don't suppose you ever do. Each day I'd tell myself not to be so stupid and tried to keep up my fitness routine.

Normally, I'd run a dozen or so laps of the local park to stay in shape. Now I couldn't manage a single lap. My legs wouldn't carry me and there was no way I could make them. The most terrifying part was going to bed at night with severe chest pains and believing that I wouldn't see the morning.

Under pressure from his wife, Karen, and his parents, Hadlee agreed to cancel his appointments for two weeks and take a holiday. His father didn't like the look of the symptoms one little bit. He doubted that his most gifted offspring would play cricket again.

The problem was where to take a holiday, and what explanation to offer to the people he had to disappoint? Being a folk hero made escaping extremely hard. The first to ask questions were his colleagues on the radio station. Once they heard, they promised to maintain a tactful silence.

Karen organised a trip to Raratonga, an idyllic Pacific hideaway in the Cook Island group; Air New Zealand cut through the red-tape and had the couple and Nicholas there in three days.

If he was expecting to get away from it all, Hadlee had another think coming. Within a few hours of arriving, they were sunbathing by the hotel swimming pool when a call came from the mainland. It was a journalist from the Eight O'clock *newspaper in Auckland, wanting to know what he was doing idling in the Pacific at that time of year. The reporter had done well to track Hadlee down and his question was legitimate enough. The answer he got doesn't stand repetition!*

I have a lot of time for the press. After all, it provides part of my living. I see absolutely no point in avoiding reporters just to be difficult. A quick quote or too and they go away happy. On this occasion, I'm afraid, I was very blunt with the guy. It was typical of my state of mind. I couldn't take any more of people wanting me to do this and do that, demanding my time on and off the field. In England, it's so much simpler—no outside engagements, just cricket then a quick beer with the lads at the end of the day and home to watch television or enjoy a take-away meal. But back home there was nowhere to hide, not even on a desert island.

It may sound a little melodramatic, but at this stage I was preoccupied with the thought of death. I was convinced I had heart trouble, which in turn made me worse. Then I was haunted by the fear of what would happen to Karen and Nicholas if my playing days were over. How could I earn the money to maintain our way of life? Anyone who's been through a breakdown must recognise the symptoms well. They may expect it of a high-powered business executive, but not a sportsman.

The goals and targets which kept me going didn't seem worth it any more. As I deteriorated, I lost faith in my own ability and doubted that I could go on achieving success — that's if I managed to pull through at all. A couple of things began to obsess me.

First was the Winsor Cup, a trophy that's presented in New Zealand each year to the best bowler. I'd won it for seven years on the trot. What would happen if I lost it? That would be the end of the world. I couldn't bear the thought of someone taking it from me. If I'd only won the cup here and there it might have been different, but I regarded it as MINE. There was some unidentifiable threat out there and it worried me sick.   Similarly, for the last few years, I'd invariably been named Man of the Series at home and abroad. I could lose that as well. The thought of someone from the opposition winning it was bad enough; the thought of one of my New Zealand team mates getting it was worse. There was so much to lose. My pride wouldn't take it and my reputation would be finished.

Karen and the family were very concerned about my state of health. The odd day was a little brighter here and there, but the majority of days were black. I'd become very drawn and lost pounds in weight. In the end, I was persuaded to see a doctor. It didn't take him long to diagnose the trouble. He told me there was only one answer — to say 'NO' to people for the foreseeable future. I'd have to be brutal and disappoint them, it was the only thing that would save me from going right downhill. Mum brought it home to me when she said that if I didn't slow down, I mightn't be around much longer!

*Hadlee's great friend and team mate, Clive Rice was one
of the few callers permitted to talk to Hadlee during this
period. Karen had put a block on all telephone calls but
she allowed her husband to take this one from
Johannesburg. Rice recalls: 'Richard sounded awful. I
hardly recognised his voice. It was as though he didn't even
have the confidence to talk.'*

*To the spectators and cricket lovers of New Zealand,
Hadlee must have seemed like the last person in the world
to break down. On the outside, he's an ultra-efficient person
who manages to be on top of most things. What they may
not fully comprehend is the pressure international players
are subjected to.*

Playing Test and first-class cricket isn't just an expenses paid
trip around the world. For us globetrotters, who leave home
to spend half the year in England, it's that much harder. Don't
misunderstand me, I wouldn't change the life, but it might
be enlightening to describe our timetable.

In order to play cricket for ten to twelve months of the year,
I have to chase the summers. The two-day flight from New
Zealand to England isn't one of my favourites. I get weary
from all the travelling, staying in hotels, packing and
unpacking bags and belongings. It's astonishing the amount
of equipment you have to take on tour. Every six months,
we have to pack up home and put most of our household
goods into store. At the end of the summer in England, the
process is repeated in reverse. As soon as I feel a 'nip' in
the air I know that the English autumn is on its way and,
like a bird, it's time to migrate. I have never seen an English
winter, and from what people tell me, I haven't missed a lot!

I've toured England three times and played in three World
Cups. I've been to India and Pakistan once each, Australia
six times and have lived and played in Tasmania for four
months. Each year I spend about four months away from
my wife and family, either playing cricket or doing
promotional work. What's more, during the English season,
county cricketers are home very little unless there's a long
sequence of home games. I'm lucky that Karen is a very
understanding wife—she once played for New Zealand

Ladies herself. But, inevitably, there's tension. What family can put up with so much separation and not feel the strain?

Being a Hadlee, I guess there was pressure on me from an early age. Dad was an international cricketer and my older brothers, Dayle and Barry have also represented their country. I suppose I was naturally expected to follow in their footsteps. The greatest pressures of all, though, are created by the public and the media. They seem to demand high quality performances day in and day out. Like any job, that's not always possible. Everywhere I go in New Zealand, and to a lesser extent in Nottingham, I'm recognised and stopped for autographs.

The day it doesn't happen is the day I'll know I'm on the way down, but in the meantime, I feel I'm being watched and must be on my best behaviour. That is true of any well-known personality, but it certainly puts restrictions on you.

When Karen and Nicholas and I were relaxing in Raratonga, I got recognised a little but not much. It surprised me that anyone should know me at all on a remote Pacific island. We had ten days of peace and quiet and it was very therapeutic.

When we got back, things started to cloud in again and within a few days of arriving home, the headaches and blurred vision returned. They weren't as acute as before, but I couldn't see any way of my recovering sufficiently to play in the forthcoming Test series against England. I could hardly bring myself to think of cricket at all and here we were, only a month away from the first Test. Unbeknown to me, my father advised the New Zealand Cricket Council about my problems and warned them that my availability was in serious doubt. They said they would leave me to make the decision.

I began to turn up to one or two practice sessions, but didn't feel at all good. There was still a lot of physical weakness and I was only coasting through — not much sign of improvement at all. The rest of the lads couldn't believe what they saw. My nature is to be positive and decisive, but I was so negative.

It's doubtful whether Hadlee would have hauled himself out of that trough in time for the England series if it hadn't been for a chance encounter with a motivation expert by the name of Grahame Felton. Felton is a cricket enthusiast who works for the Institute of Management in Christchurch, Hadlee's home town. By sheer co-incidence, he asked if he could run a course for the local Canterbury team to help prepare them mentally and physically for the start of New Zealand's domestic season. Not only did he effect a transformation in Hadlee that the doctors couldn't achieve, he actually spurred him on to more success than Hadlee imagined possible.

Over the years, several sportsmen have turned to motivationists or hypnotists to assist them over psychological hang-ups of one sort or another. The difference here is that Hadlee was not seeking that kind of help. It fell into his lap at the most opportune moment, and changed his life.

Felton's course would normally take twelve hours. For Canterbury, he decided to nip through it in three, just as an experiment. He'd never applied it to cricket before. This is Hadlee's view:

The benefits that came out of those three hours were unbelievable . . . and the timing, from my point of view, was remarkable. His method was to give us various pieces of literature to read and then to ask questions. When he discovered that I was going through traumas, he wondered if I would be his guinea pig. I said I would. What happened next was a real eye-opener to me and the rest of the team. It's not easy to recapture the mood of that session. It was intense. Grahame's message came across to me so forcibly it was like suddenly seeing the light.

There was an immediate point of contact when he began explaining how important it was to set yourself goals in life — and to stick to them through thick and thin. He was on my wavelength. Easy to say, of course, much harder to carry out those goals. I boiled it all down to a list of key words and phrases which I jotted down on a piece of card. I'd like to go through the list and explain for the benefit of those readers who might find it as helpful as I have.

The starting point is to recognise that FEAR IS

NEGATIVE. You have to rid yourself of fear and encourage the desire to be positive. Again, it's easier said than done. Some give up without really trying. One way of achieving it is through SIMULATION. That is one of the important words I came to use. It meant in my case, putting myself back in a situation in which I last enjoyed success.

I might for example be playing at Old Trafford. I'd tell myself that I did pretty well the last time I played there, taking five wickets or scoring 70 runs. With Grahame's help, I learned to play back those successes in my mind, not as if I was a spectator, but actually going through it all again in the middle. I would recreate the day in question and everything about it — the weather; the state of the game; the other players around me; whatever was occupying my mind outside the game at that particular time, etc.

The time to try that little exercise was the night before I was returning to the scene of a triumph. I'd be in the hotel room, going back over it all, MAKING it happen again. The principle is that if you've done it once, there's no reason why you shouldn't go out and repeat the performance. I'd then progress to VISUALISING what I wanted to happen this time. Obviously no-one can control the actions of other people, but I can condition myself to react in ways which will minimize their effectiveness. It could be that I was playing against Middlesex and I'd remember that the last time I faced Norman Cowans, he got me out. This time, I'd tell myself that it wouldn't happen again. Turning that around to positive thinking, I'd say to myself: 'When Cowans bowls to me tomorrow, I will stay at the crease, and when he's finished his bowling spell, I will still be batting'. Mind over matter. It works if you believe it strongly enough.

So I simulate, visualise, dream; then MAKE it happen. The point that Grahame drove home was that my mind is better than a computer and controls every single thing I do. Like a computer, the brain can be programmed to behave positively. Once it does, the body reacts accordingly.

BELIEF is another crucial factor. As with any faith, it can't work unless there is belief. I'd been doubting my ability during the illness. Now I saw how stupid it was. I had only to think back over what I'd achieved to restore my confidence.

30

Once confidence is there, success nearly always comes. Lack of confidence is a passport to failure.

How often in the past have I seen New Zealand cricketers take on England or Australia and feel beaten before they even started? Once in that frame of mind, there's little point turning up for the match. Through this course, I learned to back myself again in any given situation, no matter what the strength of the opposition or how unfavourable the conditions. I suppose it was the single most important piece of advice I picked up in overcoming my breakdown. Later, it was to help me immeasurably in achieving the 'double'.

The REWARDS of success are also a great incentive. I made myself concentrate on those. It's another stage of the self-motivation process. Winning is the most important thing, naturally, but victory usually goes hand in glove with financial bonuses, prizes, or simply the acclaim from the public and media. Those things make success all the sweeter. If getting five wickets or scoring a 100 meant earning a few more dollars too, so much the better.

TARGETS were already an essential part of my philosophy on cricket, but Grahame underlined their value. Setting targets was part of it, seeing them through, the most important part. He drilled into me the significance of wanting to prove myself better than the opposition — not just now and then, but every time. His lesson had an immediate salutory effect on me because I won the Winsor Cup I'd been so worried about losing. It ended up on my sideboard for the eighth successive year. A local magazine report suggested that they should award the trophy to me permanently, because I 'monopolised the show'. I don't mind reports like that! Winning it again was purely down to attitude. I was determined to outdo my opponents and prove myself the best.

Beating the opponent became a driving force. More often than not, the opponent was Botham. I had a fixation about it. He was the one I had to beat, whether with wickets or runs. In the 1984 series in New Zealand I beat him easily on the wickets, but he edged me out with the runs.

I turned that England series into a personal duel between Botham and me. It was part of the positive-thinking programme. In our team talk before the First Test, I suggested to the players that they should pick an opponent out of the England ranks and set themselves the target of bettering his performance throughout the series. Our two opening batsmen took Tavare and Smith or Fowler; I took Botham; Ian Smith took Bob Taylor and so on. At the end of the three Tests, we compared the performances of ourselves and our opposite numbers. Invariably, most of our guys beat the opponent with ease. I figured that if we each won our own personal battle, we were bound to beat England as a team. I must have sounded like Grahame Felton himself in the dressing room. I'd gained so much from him that I wanted to share the experience with the rest of the team.

WANTING to achieve was the next stage in the formula. Desire for success has never eluded me — quite the opposite. Sometimes I probably drive people mad with it. Grahame reinforced that part of my mental attitude too. Winning Test matches, or Wimbledon, or the Open golf, or any major sporting event isn't necessarily about the man or woman with most talent. He or she has a hell of a start on the others, but everyone competing has it within them to win. They all have ability or they wouldn't be there in the first place. The winners are those who know how to maximise it. They WANT to win so badly that they do. It doesn't always make them popular. John McEnroe is a prime example. But then popularity isn't the name of the game.

Another key word I made a note of on my famous piece of cardboard was CONTROL. This refers to the way you have to convert all your dreaming and visualising into physical action. Very important. The body has to work in tune with the mind. With both working in unision, you have cracked it. In simple terms, that translates as doing your running, your exercises and preparing yourself in the nets. This is only preparation of course. What really matters is doing your stuff out there in the middle. There are a few players I could name who might benefit from a course like this. Players who look world-class in practice or lesser games, but 'freeze' when it comes to the big occasion. How many promising careers have been ruined in cricket and soccer because a talented individual couldn't produce the goods when it mattered — couldn't CONTROL his ability?

ENJOYMENT is the next part of the equation. This can easily be overlooked. I must admit that it doesn't come easily to me even now. At the highest level, that is Test match level, I can honestly say I enjoy having success and being out there with a big crowd urging me on, or even urging the opposition on. Away from that arena, cricket can become just another job.

Grahame convinced me about the robot element in all of us. What he means is that everyone has a tape recorder inside them. Like any other tape recorder, you can press the rewind button and relive the good times. The bad ones you must erase. If anything negative comes into your mind, throw it out. On the odd occasion when I thought I might be struggling to reach the double, I discarded those thoughts through sheer willpower and got back into the attack. Another one of his catchphrases is . . . Never get tired, just PLEASANTLY WEARY. If you walk off the pitch thinking and saying that you're shattered, you will be. It's a negative thing. You should convince yourself instead that you're only pleasantly weary. That's positive thinking.

And to finish with, a thought which sums up my whole attitude. Winning is being HAPPY WITH YOUR OWN PERFORMANCE, even though someone might have done better than you. As long as I know I have given one hundred per cent, it doesn't matter so much if I haven't quite achieved what I was after. Let me give you an example. At the end of the cricket season, Clive Rice won the Silk Cut All-Rounders competition at Taunton.

He was up against Botham, Malcolm Marshall, Kapil Dev and myself, so, with Imran Khan injured it was the unofficial world title. It hurt to lose but I consoled myself with the thought that I had done the best I could and, on the day, Clive was better than me. On another day, I will be better than him. You must accept certain things that you can't control. Once the day's over, there's nothing you can do to change anything. I have had my share of failures and a lot of successes too. Mixed in there as well is a pinch or two of mediocrity.

It was at the end of December 1983 when Hadlee wrote out the motivation card which has become his Bible. He

33

has carried it in his cricket bag ever since, and won't travel anywhere without it.

I just throw the lid up and there it sits, staring at me. I don't use it every day because I know it by heart. When things go wrong and I need something to lift my spirits, I pull out the card and go through it again. It inspires me. It gets me simulating and visualising all over again and it's become a very important part of my life.

Within a week or so of Grahame's course, I started to feel much better. The desire to get up and do something came back. Most important, the desire to play cricket and achieve more success came rushing back and once that happened, most other things fell into place. In order to get back into action, I had to condition myself all over again. That meant resuming the running and fitness training that I'd abandoned. I went to the park again and forced myself to run one lap. It would normally take me seven minutes. This time it took thirteen. I was barely moving but that didn't matter. The important thing was that I got round, something I could never have done a few weeks before.

Things started to progress. I had only two weeks before the season opened. The headaches had subsided and the dizziness was gone. My eyes still felt a little heavy but much better than they had been, the chest pains were a thing of the past and over a period of one week, my recovery had come on in leaps and bounds.

I kept working every day, doing a bit more each time, reducing my lap times around the park. By the time of the first game I was still some way off proper fitness. My mind was back in business, but I needed more sharpening up. Even so, I had some reasonable successes in the domestic competition, scoring 90-odd and taking four wickets in the first match. On the strength of that, I told the Council I WOULD be available for the England series.

Grahame Felton's influence spread to Hadlee's Canterbury team mates, the ones he'd used in that short motivation course. The side started off in tremendous form at home, winning the first two first-class matches and the opening two one-day games. Away from home, things weren't so

34

impressive. When Hadlee left for the Sri Lanka tour, Canterbury were knocked out of the limited over competition but hit a purple patch towards the end of the season, coming from nowhere to win the championship. Hadlee had no doubts where the inspiration came from.

It was all down to Grahame. Imagine his delight and the delight of the team when they lifted that trophy. What a great example it was for him. I cannot thank him enough. Throughout that following summer in England, he and I were in regular contact. When I achieved the double, I thanked him personally over the airwaves for his help. Part of my success was his and I wanted him to know that.

4

Double or Quit

Ken Taylor, the Notts manager breathed a sigh of relief when Hadlee landed back on English soil. The annual uncertainty was over. Notts were far from a one-man band, but Hadlee could make all the difference to another challenge for honours. Just having him there was an inspiration to the younger players, many of whom had been gathered from the club's doorstep.

This year there was a change of address for the Hadlees. Taylor had found them a detached Victorian house to rent, only a mile or so from the ground. Slowly they began the laborious business of unpacking, settling in again and preparing for a long, hard season.

The weather continued to be remarkably good for springtime. First visitors to Trent Bridge in 1984 were Surrey, a team against which Hadlee expected to do well. His budget said so! Notts were on their toes — Clive Rice had impressed on his team the importance of winning games early in the season while the sun still shone. May was traditionally wet, so a win in April could be worth its weight in gold.

Notts DID win — and comfortably. Thanks to Rice (48), they totalled 175 in their first innings after deciding to bat. Hadlee contributed only 11, batting at number seven and failed to get to the crease a second time. He had only himself to blame — and the young off-spinner Peter Such! Both took eight wickets in the match as Surrey were dismissed for 129 and 148. Hadlee was immediately in the *groove, claiming 4—8 in the first innings and a further 4—14 in the second. What a start to his 'double' effort! This was the first game both sides had played under the new regulation that 117 overs were to be bowled each day.*

Another fine, dry day greeted the club's second match of the season, against David Gower's Leicestershire at Trent Bridge. Gower, the man who would lead England that summer missed the game because of a septic finger. In his absence, Peter Willey invited Notts to bat, but Hadlee missed the chance to improve his run aggregate. He was caught off Jonathan Agnew for 14, though he made 25 not out second time around.

It was a thin time with the ball for Hadlee too. He failed to take a wicket in his opening spell when Leicestershire replied to the Notts first innings total of 291. In his second spell, he had Mike Garnham taken behind the wicket and clean bowled Agnew for an analysis of 2—68 off twenty-four overs. His twenty overs in the Leicestershire second innings didn't produce a wicket and the game fizzled out into a draw.

The summer's first rain interrupted the second day of the next championship game at Headingley. Yorkshire, under the captaincy of David Bairstow scored 301—5 declared with Hadlee's least favourite adversary, Boycott run out for 73. Yorkshire went on to win the match in a somewhat contrived fashion after Rice had declared the Notts first innings at 36—3. Hadlee had hit a dry spell in the wet — only one run and one wicket to show for his efforts. It meant that after three games he was behind target with 51 runs and 11 wickets. He wasn't worried about the bowling:

I knew that if I bowled something like 700 overs, I'd get 100 wickets. It wasn't so much the number of games as the number of overs that was important. It worked out about right. I was striking about every seven overs. The batting worried me a little at this stage. I was only getting niggly scores and down at number seven, there was a good chance I wouldn't get two cracks of the whip every time.

Before long, he would be moved up the order to number six, but it was never easy knowing quite where to play him.

37

Says his manager, Ken Taylor:

' The snag was, Richard would never take his batting that seriously. I always thought he was a fine batsman, but he wouldn't get down to it. I often pulled his leg and told him that with a little more concentration he would get many bigger scores. I remember his magnificent 142 not out at Bradford in 1981 on a nasty wicket with Alan Ramage bowling exceptionally well for Yorkshire. We were really struggling but Richard got his head down and resisted his usual temptation to have a whack. At lunch he said to me: "Bloody hell this is hard work! Is it always like this?"

'I told him the foundation he'd built would pay off in the second part of the innings and sure enough, after lunch, he hit the ball all over Yorkshire! One of his problems is that he sometimes feels it's the recognised batsmen's job to get the runs, not his. Rather like Gary Sobers, he sets himself very high standards and has trouble understanding people who don't play to their full potential.'

Hadlee sees it this way:

I don't feel as though I'm necessarily in control when I'm batting . . . only perhaps 60% of the time. Early on I'm very tentative, likely to play a big shot and loft it, which is not what a genuine batsman would do. It's different once I get to 15 or 20. Then I start to feel in control.

I much prefer bowling. That's my art. I'm in control 95% of the time. It's the bowler who dictates the play, unless someone like Viv Richards comes along. Wherever the bowler pitches the ball dictates whether runs are scored and where. One of the key phrases I picked up from Grahame Felton was that I'M the one who will do the testing, I will not let anyone test ME.

Off my shortened run, I found that I was more effective than I've ever been. I can still bowl bouncers and stick guys on their backsides, but nowadays, I don't mind batsmen coming forward and driving me through the covers. I can push them back and deceive them with change of pace, by switching to round the wicket, and using all the variations that have now become my greatest asset. The quicker ball is still as quick as it was off the twenty metre run-up, but of course, it doesn't come as often. That's a good thing because the batsman gets used to me bowling at a certain pace, then all of a sudden—whoosh—he's fending at the quick one and gloving it or miscuing or getting a knock in the ribs. Very few of them see it coming and that's when our slip fielders have to be aware. A nick off one of those will reach them shoulder high.

My basic ball is a leg-cutter, hitting the seam and nipping away to the slips. By coming wider of the crease, I can also produce the one that nips back. I don't swing the ball a lot though the faster one tends to leave the batsman. My favourite is the 'dangly', the slower one which does swing as long as I pitch it right up. There's enough there to keep the batsman guessing. The average over is made up of four leg-cutters, just short of a length. The 'dangly' would come every second over; the flier once an over and I'd throw a shorter one in every now and then. The secret is not to overdo it. I may have slung down three bouncers in three overs, but in the fourth over, when they might be expecting another, I'd fire one straight into the block hole.

I'm not necessarily thinking of each ball I'm bowling, rather of the over as a whole. It's like a gun that's got six shells. Four of them might not be designed to get the batsman out. They could be pushing him onto the back foot, setting him up for the fifth which will be completely different. That's the great joy of bowling . . . dominating the man at the other end, making him worry so that pyschologically I have him where I want him. Far from making a big score, he's more intent on survival. Most county batsmen will try to see me off instead of chasing me. That means they have to chance their arm against the bowler from the other end, and he, in turn picks up wickets.

Dennis Lillee is my idol. He's the epitome of fast bowling. The times I've actually sat down and chatted with him are few. You don't get opportunities like that with the Aussies. If you're ever with them at a function of some sort, they're always the first to leave and don't seem keen to talk for very long. I don't remember Lillee ever coming into our dressing room though if you ever do get near to him, you find him a likeable and easy-going sort of bloke. Once he gets on that field he's a fierce competitor. That's what I like.

He doesn't know this, but I've got miles of video tape of Lillee at home and spend hours studying his style. Some people think they can see a similarity in our actions. I wouldn't know about that, but if it's true, it's not surprising. There's certainly a similarity of approach. I share the same key motives as Lillee — off-stump line; hate; desire to get rid of the batsman because he's an obstacle; rhythm, timing, co-ordination.

Lillee is a superb athlete. To come back from a serious back injury took some guts. I admire that. People wrote him off a few times, but he always proved them wrong. He was a matchwinner who could lift a whole team. When things aren't going so well for me, I often ask myself what Lillee would do in this situation. The answer always comes back, he wouldn't give up. Clive knows he only has to mention Lillee to me and it fires me up. He's unquestionably the best bowler there's been.

Botham will beat him statistically but to me there's no comparison. I never saw Trueman but it's hard to imagine anyone better than Lillee. In unison with Thommo he was a frightening sight. His Test record would have been even more impressive if he hadn't been isolated for three years because of World Series. His Test figures are by no means a true representation of his quality. He picked up eighty unofficial Test wickets which would have brought his total to 430 — that's 123 more than Trueman.

Lillee's aggression has got the better of him here and there, but that's understandable. Controversial incidents are inevitable with bowlers like that. I've had a few myself. There's nothing wrong with a verbal duel between the batsman and the bowler. It's a battle of wits and in a sense, all's fair. Lillee did it, so did Trueman. The purpose is to break the batsman's concentration and induce him to make a mistake. Once that happens, the bowler and fielders cash in on the lapse and seize the initiative. The Aussies are the masters.

Critics say it's gamesmanship and that it brings cricket into disrepute. I don't believe there's any malice intended. You've got to have played cricket at that level to understand how frustrations build up and how the bowler has to let off steam.

Lillee's famous kick at Javed Miandad in the Pakistan series is not to be condoned, but I can understand what he must have been feeling. Javed is a cheeky little player, always trying to annoy and goad the fielders. His favourite trick is to stand outside the crease and invite the close fielders to throw down his stumps. Lillee was fined 200 dollars for the kick, but probably felt it was worthwhile. He said he believed in 'an eye for an eye' and I can't help but agree. Where I draw the line is pursuing a personal grievance in a public place. Perhaps he should have sorted it out after the game.

The aluminium bat incident was another case in point. I believe Lillee was asking for trouble using the bat in a Test match, and Mike Brearley was probably quite right to protest. Lillee was after publicity for the bat and certainly got it! That was wrong.

It's a pity that it did more harm than good in the end because the aluminium bat was banned. I think there is a place for it in cricket. It's a great learning tool for kids and doesn't crack or split like a wooden bat. Willow is so expensive for kids these days that I wouldn't be surprised to see Lillee's piece of metal making a reappearance somewhere.

Hadlee's statistics may not place him in the list of alltime top wicket takers. Being a New Zealander, he hasn't had the number of matches to compare with Botham. That is a shame and, given his predilection for records, will surely irk him well after retirement.

It should be a great consolation to him that he would come close to the top of most people's lists of great fast bowlers, and would be a certainty in most World Elevens. Clive Rice has played with or against most of the best quickies of modern times and has no doubts about Hadlee's ranking:

'He is absolutely brilliant. I rate him alongside Dennis Lillee and that is about the finest tribute you could have. They are the two most skilled bowlers I've ever seen, and both had the capacity to be as fast as anyone in the world. The West Indians

41

are consistently faster, but Hadlee and Lillee belong to a different category. They are advanced bowlers.

'Fielding to Richard's bowling is tough. If you think he gets batsmen in trouble, you want to know what it's like in the slips! We just don't know when the "flier" is coming. I've watched him for seven years now, and I'm none the wiser. It's so well disguised. We might get three catches in a day. Perhaps one will be a flier and the other two will be the "dangly". Lose concentration for a moment, and you will miss it. Then you're in trouble. He hates giving runs away. The team's petrified of misfielding or dropping a catch!

'Early on in the 1984 season he dropped a slip catch off my bowling. It struck him in the chest and went down. Mad?—not likely, I was delighted! During the next few months, I knew I was bound to do the same to him and now I wouldn't feel so bad about it.

'I can only recall him getting a pasting once in all my time at Notts. It was a Sunday League match at Trent Bridge in 1983 and Richards and Botham were racing each other to the hundred. I threw Richard the ball to break the partnership and said: "I look forward to the contest!" The batsmen were going like trains and Richard got some stick like everyone else. Apart from those two, I can't think of anyone else who could dish out that treatment to him.

'Being on the same side as Richard has been my great fortune. I've had to face him only a couple of times, for T. N. Pearce's Eleven, and the All-Rounder competition at Taunton, apart from in the nets. Believe me, I'm grateful to have got off so lightly!'

Chelmsford has more than once been a happy hunting ground for Hadlee. In his budget, the Essex match was detailed as a possible bonanza fixture . . . another opportunity for runs and wickets. Towards the end of May, the weather had turned cooler and damp. Before the heavens opened at 3 p.m., Notts had completed a 10 wicket victory over the team which would pip them to the championship title more than three months later.

Keith Fletcher won the toss and Notts batted. Broad and Robinson went in quick succession to the pace of John

42

Lever and Neil Foster but Randall and Rice spearheaded a Notts recovery on a wicket offering help to the pacemen. A wet outfield made life extra difficult for the batsmen. Randall had defied the Essex attack for 145 minutes, scoring 56 when Hadlee stepped in for his assault.

A typical, bludgeoning innings of 71 not out helped Notts to reach 264 and boosted his run tally at last. Kevin Saxelby and Rice did most of the damage when the reigning champions came to bat. Essex managed a meagre 93 all out, of which Gooch made 33. Rice took 3 – 15; Saxelby claimed four wickets without conceding a run to finish with 4 – 15, and Hadlee had to be content with one victim, Lever, caught in the slips.

When Essex followed on, Hadlee swiftly removed Chris Gladwin but Gooch was in imperious form. We were to see many performances like this from him before the season was out, and it seemed that Notts' victory prospects were extinguished. With Fletcher, Gooch added 167 for the second wicket. The second day closed with Essex 186 – 2. Next morning, Saxelby dislodged Fletcher for 83, Gooch for 108 and David East for 16. From 228 – 5, the home side collapsed to 257 all out in Hadlee's brilliant burst of 5 – 11 in five overs.

That gave me seven wickets in the match and was a real bonus. I had great pleasure filling in my score chart after that game.

To the amazement of his county colleagues, Hadlee would sit in the dressing room after a match, surrounded by papers and folders, more like an accountant than a cricketer. Here was a man who'd played cricket at the highest level all around the world, filling in his log like an enthusiastic schoolboy. More than once his team mates wondered, but never asked, where the motivation came from. How did he produce his best day after day in front of the merest handful of spectators? If they'd asked, this would have been his answer:

Pride of performance is my motivation. Just because you're a Test player, it doesn't mean that you should drop your standards when you play in a lesser grade of cricket. Other players in the team expect you to perform, they look up to you and if they see you're not trying, that's hardly going to stimulate them. They wouldn't respect me for it. I give my best in any type of cricket because it's the only way I know how to play. I can't stand failure.

The first time I tasted it was in 1967 when I failed the school certificate. I was sixteen at the time and the aim was to get a 200 pass mark in your four best subjects. I'll never forget the letter coming in the mail and Mum bringing it to me on a silver platter. I opened it only to discover that I'd got 195 and failed. It was degrading, embarrassing and very depressing. The following year, I sat the examination again and passed in every subject. I constantly look back on that example. Ever since I've detested failure and believed that success was the only way.

Even on a miserable day with nobody watching the game I have no difficulty galvanising myself into action. I like to look at the newspaper next day and see confirmed that I've taken another five wickets or whatever to help my tally. It's a bit like a company with its financial year and its balance sheet. Half way through the year, or at the end you take stock to see if you are in the 'red or black', or ahead of budget. If you're in the red there's something wrong. You've got to analyse the situation and isolate the problem. If you're in the black, whether it's money, wickets or runs, you're a success. It's as simple as that.

I'd be lying if I said I wasn't spurred on by big crowds. We only get those in the one-day games, so there's no use moaning about it. Crowds can obviously inspire you. We had a crowd revolution in New Zealand cricket when we played Australia in 1977. The second new ball had arrived in the Auckland Test and was given to me. I probably had 0 – 90 at the time. The first ball Rod Marsh played and missed. Next ball, the same. The third hit him on the pad – out lbw and there was a real buzz in the stands. Gary Gilmour came in and missed the first ball he received. The crowd was roaring: 'Had – lee, Had – lee' and the beer cans were clattering. I'd never had that before. It had never happened in the history of New Zealand cricket.

44

That's when people started to say that I'd become a folk hero. The support I had that day at Eden Park was amazing. It lifted me but it drained me as well. I'd be running into bowl in tune with the chanting and putting in the extra bit of effort. Suddenly, because I was trying so hard, my strength would give out. After a few eight ball overs, I had to rest. Crowd support of that magnitude is one of the rewards of success, one of the things over and above what you'd normally get out of a daily cricket routine. It's something to cherish because it doesn't happen very often.

The fifth and sixth matches of the season were not very productive. Hadlee collected a couple of wickets and 10 runs at Derby and nothing at Edgbaston. Things picked up against Hampshire at Bournemouth where the century he badly needed duly arrived. It took him 159 minutes and provided his captain with the impetus to push for victory. Coming in at 134−5, Hadlee set about the Hampshire attack with such relish that Notts were able to declare their first innings at 308−5, five runs ahead. Hadlee was firing on all cylinders now. With Mike Hendrick making one of his rare appearances, the pair whipped out the opposition for 127 second time around. Hendrick took 5−17, Hadlee 5-35.

At one point in the proceedings, Rice had dropped out of the slips because of his broken finger. Eddie Hemmings, not a noted close fielder, had to deputise at first slip. One 'snick' hit Hemmings on the wrist before he could react, a second whistled past his shoulder like a bullet. Hadlee stormed over to Rice and bellowed: 'Get that clown out of there!' For the rest of the innings, Rice, broken finger and all, was in the firing line having moved Eddie to third slip. Richard couldn't work that one out.

Chasing only 123 for another win, Notts plummetted to 49−5 before Hadlee came in. Taylor recalls:
'We had Hampshire by the throat, but could easily have lost that match disgracefully. Richard was beginning to realise that our batting, despite all the names we had, was as unreliable as ever. If he'd been worried about not getting enough innings to reach the 1,000 runs target, it must have dawned on him at that point that he needn't have feared.

45

Thanks to him and French we won that game. Others may not have been giving 100%, but that was never a problem with Richard. When it's boring and there's no prospect of a result, he might lose a little interest, but if he sees others responding, he'll always support their efforts.'

The Hampshire game was an important milestone for Hadlee:

It took my run aggregate from 132 to 232, still behind target, but it gave me the encouragement to keep going. Moving to six in the order was a good fillip as well. I never lost the position after that.

The eighth championship game of the season brought Glamorgan to Trent Bridge in glorious sunshine at the beginning of June. It was another crushing 10 wicket win which gave Notts a further twenty-two points and hoisted them to second place in the Britannic Assurance table. Leicestershire had 109 points, Notts 106. Overwhelming victories like that weren't a lot of use to Hadlee in his run chase. With only one innings, he had to make a big score first time to stay on target. As it happened, he scored a typically quickfire 71 in the Notts innings of 349−8 declared.

It was a turning wicket on which Eddie Hemmings proved the most effective bowler, taking six wickets in each innings. Hadlee had another four to add to his list.

After a third of the season I had 340 runs when I really hoped for 400. Four times in those first eight games I didn't bat, so I was deprived of those. If it continued that way, I could see there was a chance I wouldn't make it. The wickets were behind schedule as well. I had 31 when my budget was 40, but we had plenty of games left at Trent Bridge so I wasn't unduly concerned.

5

Beating The Poms . . . Part I

Trent Bridge had marked an important milestone in Richard Hadlee's career. During the fourth and final Test against England the previous summer, he joined the exclusive club of all-rounders who have taken 200 Test wickets. It was fitting that he should have accomplished that feat in front of a Nottingham audience.

Willis and Lamb were batting on the fourth morning of the Test with England 252 − 8. It was Sunday and Trent Bridge was nicely full. Willis had surprised us by not enforcing the follow-on when New Zealand were on the rack. He took the decision presumably to prolong the match into Sunday when the gate receipts would be vital.

So, only two England wickets left and I needed them both to reach the 200. The pressure was on. My first few overs had proved fairly expensive and when the second new ball arrived, I had visions of Geoff Howarth resting me. Luckily he didn't. I decided to come around the wicket to 'Goose' who was starting to frustrate me. The plan paid immediate dividends. The first ball lifted his leg stump out of the ground to make it 199. Dad was over for the series and he'd advised me the night before to bowl round the wicket to the lower order batsmen − still a good judge isn't he?

Norman Cowans was last man in. I went back over the wicket to him. With the last ball of my twenty-eighth over, I uprooted his off stump and achieved another dream. I stood in the middle of the pitch showing no emotion. All I felt was relief and thankfulness. It had taken me twelve years of Test cricket, 44 Tests and 11,000 deliveries — not to mention a helluva lot of blood sweat and tears!

I kept the ball as a memento and walked through the members stand applauded by players and supporters. It was very moving. Bob Willis was at the dressing room door to congratulate me. A fine tribute from a fine cricketer. Dad was speechless. He just reached out and shook my hand.

The Trent Bridge Test was a memorable one for reasons apart from my 200 wickets. It brought into conflict two local lads on their home pitch — Derek Randall and myself. Derek won hands down. I guess he was named in the side to increase the size of the gate. Notts supporters might well have rioted if their hero had been left out! My goodness, how Derek repaid the selectors and the cricket lovers of the East Midlands.

The pitch was an absolute beauty. Ron Allsop, the groundsman wasn't going to do me any favours by preparing his usual fast, grassy track. That was alright for county championship games, but not for a Test. It was brown and bare and looked full of runs. Ron's reputation was at stake after all the stick he'd taken about preparing 'result' wickets in our championship-winning season.

If there was pressure on him, and on Derek, there was pressure on me too. A lot of support would come from the Trent Bridge faithful but most of them would be on Derek's side, naturally. He's the local hero, not me. I was determined to win the confrontation. Although Derek's a friend, I badly wanted to 'roll him over'. For the time being, HE, not Botham, was enemy number one.

We lost the toss and fielded all day — heartbreaking for us, but great news for the crowd which enjoyed a marvellous spectacle. England's batting was some of the finest I've ever seen. Gower took a nasty blow on the head, but bravely carried on to make 72. You had to admire him for that, though he had been a real thorn in our side. What came next set the place alight. England were 169 — 5 when Botham and Randall turned the game on its head.

Each batsman had reached his half century when Botham suddenly switched into a different gear. He flayed our attack

48

Concentration, determination and rhythm

MOTIVATION { FEAR IS NEGATIVE
DESIRE IS POSITIVE. }

- YOUR MIND IS YOUR BRAIN - IT IS BETTER THAN A COMPUTER
- ATTITUDE IS FRAME OF MIND.
- SIMULATION - PUT YOURSELF IN SITUATION WHEN YOU LAST DID IT
- VISUALISE - DREAM + KNOW YOU CAN DO IT.
- BELIEVE - CONFIDENCE BREEDS SUCCESS.
- THINK OF THE REWARDS OF SUCCESS - WINNING.
- SELF ESTEEM - KNOW YOUR OWN WORTH /ABILITY/VALUE.
- GOALS, AIMS, TARGETS. - BE BETTER THAN OPPOSITION - BEAT OPPONENT
- YOU MUST WANT TO DO IT - POWER OF POSITIVE THINKING
- CONTROL - CONVERT MENTAL INTO PHYSICAL /ACTIONS.
- ENJOYMENT. (I'LL DO THE TESTING - I WON'T BE TESTED)
- ROBOT - RECORD, + REPLAY THE GOOD THINGS -
- NEVER GET TIRED - JUST PLEASANTLY WEARY.
- WINNING IS BEING HAPPY WITH WITH YOUR PERFORMANCE
EVEN IF SOMEONE DOES IT BETTER.

Recipe for success. 'The motivation card that has become my bible'

The crowd at Lancaster Park, Christchurch, with a message for England's selectors

Sorry reading for England as history is made at Christchurch, 1984

*Champagne screen! Geoff Howarth and the boys at long last explode England's invincibility —
Headingley 1983*

Profile of a fast bowler. Who needs a long run-up?

'Most of the things said about Ian Botham and myself are true. The rivalry is deadly'

'"Rags" Derek Randall: predictable only at being unpredictable!'

'I felt for David Gower . . . playing your first series as captain against the West Indies is a nightmare'

'Full of menace. Dennis Lillee is everything a fast bowler could hope to be'

'Norman Cowans deserves better treatment. He's the only genuine paceman England have got'

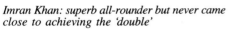

Imran Khan: superb all-rounder but never came close to achieving the 'double'

'Now that fast bowlers have worked out how to bowl to Gower, his career has changed dramatically'

'England badly needs Graham Gooch — but plonking that left foot down the pitch can be a weakness'

'At my stage, I don't want to be running five miles a day. I do enough to keep in trim'

Put it there pal! Hadlee reunited with Glenn Turner, the great trailblazer of New Zealand cricket

as only he can. There was nothing I nor anyone else could do about it. His second 50 arrived in twenty-six minutes. Derek was going like a bomb too. He played a majestic innings, stroking me through the covers off the front and back foot and seldom looking in trouble. He was aiming for the century he wanted so badly in front of his home crowd. It was a great shame he didn't quite get it.

He was only 17 runs short when, for some reason best known to himself, he went for a cover drive, failed to get to the pitch and was caught by Bruce Edgar for 83. It was his only chance to shine for England that summer, but within a few months, Randall would have more punishment in store for New Zealand.

The damage was done. England finished the day at 362 – 7 in 100 overs and we had to grin and bear it. On that form, there was no answer to Botham or Randall. My feeling was: 'That's another day at the office completed – not a good day, but a bit closer to retirement or being fired!'

In the tavern afterwards, I went for a lager or two with the members. I knew I'd take a ribbing from them for my figures of 1 – 80 from twenty-three overs. Derek had got the better of me and it hurt, but I couldn't let it show. After the second lager, it didn't seem so bad! I consoled myself with the thought that he'd been slightly lucky when he was on 12, miscuing an attempted pull which just failed to give me a caught-and-bowled. 'Arkle' and I were destined to meet again in the second innings. He wasn't in such convincing form then. Again, there was a terrific buzz of excitement around Trent Bridge as I came in to bowl to him. The buzz quickly turned to a groan when Derek's off peg came flying out of the ground. Two balls later I bowled Bob Taylor to leave me chasing those last two wickets for my 200.

We needed 511 to win that Test and square the series at 2 – 2. Not much hope of that, although, personally speaking, the match still had something to offer. I'd taken 21 wickets in the series to beat Tony MacGibbon's New Zealand record set in 1958, but I needed a good innings to improve my chances of being 'Man of the Series'. In addition, I wanted as many runs as possible to get nearer to my target of the Test 'double' of 2,000 runs and 200 wickets. Only Richie

Benaud, Sir Gary Sobers, Ian Botham, Kapil Dev and Imran Khan had done it. With 508 runs to go, I was struggling to make it that day.

However, 92 not out was very useful. It lifted my batting average for the series to 50, my best performance in twelve years. Once again targets had proved my greatest motivation.

We lost the Test heavily and with it the series. It was a terrible let-down after our sterling efforts at Headingley which was without any question, the greatest achievement in the history of New Zealand cricket. To beat England on their own soil — you can't do better than that.

History will probably record that the eleven who took part in that win were a great team. On the day, we were. Whether it was the best-ever New Zealand team I'm not sure. What I do know is that we were fighting in that Test for all the teams which had gone before us and failed. Victory was for them as much as for us. You only had to see the look on Dad's face to appreciate that. I'm so pleased he was there to witness it.

I look back on the game with a mixture of pleasure and pain. I bowled forty-seven overs at Headingley, and didn't take a wicket. It's the first time in my Test career this had happened. It wasn't that I bowled badly. Some of the commentators said I was the pick of the bowlers, despite my analysis. The rest of the lads pulled my leg something awful, telling me I was only in the team because of my batting etc. I guess it happens to us all some time. I remembered how Dennis Lillee failed to get a wicket against us at the Melbourne Cricket Ground, while I was getting nine. I tried not to take it too hard, but I was determined to come back and prove to everyone that I hadn't finished taking Test wickets.

Lance Cairns bowled beautifully in the English first innings, taking 7—74 and beating the previous best New Zealand performance in England only one Test match after it had been achieved. I'd taken 6—53 to establish a new record only a few days earlier in the Oval Test. Funnily enough, Lance nearly didn't play in the match. He'd been out of form and was given a last chance against Warwickshire before the Test. He took seven wickets there, but could never have dreamed of repeating the dose at Headingley.

There was no sign of a collapse when Tavare and Lamb added 100 for the third wicket after we'd disposed of Fowler and Gower. We'd worked out our tactics for Gower, and for the third successive time, he fell to the off-stump ploy, Coney taking the slip catch off Cairns.

The game swung back our way when England lost Lamb and Botham in the session before tea, Lamb had made 58, but Botham was the danger man. He looked in deadly form and blasted 19 off one over from Chatfield. We all knew what Botham had done against the Aussies on this very ground! Fortunately, before his innings was in full flow, Cairns got one to leave him and the skipper took a good catch at first slip. That was a relief! Still, at 175 − 4, we all felt that England had taken control of the game, and that our decision to put them in had been a bad one.

We couldn't have been more wrong! Instead of looking at a total of 300 or more, we had the Poms all out for 225. Their last six wickets went for only 50 runs after tea, thanks mainly to Cairns' magnificent swing bowling. I sent down twenty-one overs for 44 runs, but apart from beating the bat on several occasions, had nothing else to show for it. I felt I had Lamb out lbw but the umpire didn't agree. The fact was that the pitch was perfect for medium pace seam and swing. It suited Cairns, Coney and Chatfield down to the ground. Perhaps England had miscalculated in their team selection. Willis, Dilley and Cowans were too fast to exploit it fully. Only Botham had the ideal pace. He could have been a real threat.

Wright and Martin Crowe got us off to a terrific start, after 'Bootsie' Edgar retired hurt with a painful blow on the hip. We might have pressed home the advantage if it hadn't been for two tragic run-outs. Wright pushed a ball to mid-off and started to run. Geoff Howarth came for the single but Wright sent him back. Lamb swooped on the ball and threw down the wicket from 15 yards. Howarth was out for 13 and much of the good work could have been undone. Worse was to follow when Jeff Crowe was run out without scoring after Wright had sent him back too. Two run-outs at that stage of the innings was criminal.

What a day it had been for 'Shake' Wright. His 93 had been a great knock for us, but the run-outs rather blotted his copybook. What's more, he had to confess when he came in that he'd been bursting to relieve himself at the crease and couldn't contain it. He had no alternative but to 'go to the toilet' in the middle of the field. Our poor old dressing room attendant had the unenviable job of washing his underpants and jock strap!

We sank to 218 − 5, but Edgar was back at the crease and going well. He and I saw out the day with New Zealand on 252 − 5, a lead of 27. Botham hadn't turned out to be the hazard we imagined. He didn't bowl very well. Willis did, but used himself only in short bursts. Cowans was probably the most impressive of the England attack. By close of play, I'd reached my second half-century of the series. It wasn't a typical knock. The bowlers refused to pitch the ball up, preferring to drop just short of a length. They were good tactics, because I wasn't allowed the room to launch a proper offensive.

Then to the all-important third day when we HAD to get a lead of around 150 to make a push for victory. For that, we required a sound start. Edgar and I stayed for the first hour, and I went on to make 75. I had visions of reaching my second Test hundred, but Cowans forced me into error with a short ball which I tried to pull through a fairly vacant leg side. To my horror, I played the ball onto my wicket. My innings had lasted three hours. Normally if I'd managed to bat for that long, I'd have had 150 against my name!

Edgar was eventually bowled by Willis, but we achieved our target of a 150-run lead with the help of some lusty hitting from Cairns. He walloped Edmonds for two 6's and a couple of 4's.

We were looking for the early break-through when England batted a second time. They made a sound enough start, although Tavare was very streaky. My bad luck with the ball continued. I had both openers dropped. It was Chatfield who brought the first success when he produced a ball which kept low to Tavare and removed his off stump. Soon, the captain brought Coney into the attack with immediate results. Lamb and Gower had put on 72 when Lamb tried to cut an inswinger and edged it onto his wicket. 'Mantis' certainly had his thinking cap on. He'd bowled Lamb a series of out-swingers and took him totally by surprise with the one which came into him.

Botham's wicket was another boost. He'd survived an appeal for a bat-pad catch off the first ball, smashed the second for four through the covers, then was out. Trying to sweep the third ball from Coney, Botham top-edged behind the wicket-keeper and Howarth took the catch.

England 126−4, still 26 runs behind with four top batsmen in the pavilion. Derek Randall was playing well but Chatfield had him caught behind by Smith−the third time he'd been dismissed in exactly the same fashion. At stumps, England were 154−6, a lead of only two. There were still two days left for us to wrap up the innings. Our problem was Gower. We had to restrict him as much as possible because the last thing we wanted was to be chasing much more than fifty to sixty runs. On a deteriorating wicket, runs would be hard to come by in the fourth innings. We had a whole day to think about it, as Sunday was a rest day. I went back to Notts to be with the family. It rained during the afternoon and I harboured dark thoughts.

What if we let it slip now? The weather forecast wasn't good. It would be a tragedy if we were denied our chance to create history. Ten years earlier, I recalled having Australia 30−2 in their second innings, chasing 400. It rained for two days and they were saved. Surely the fates wouldn't be so unkind? Then I thought about a similar situation two years earlier at Headingley when Australia were apparently home and dry. Players and press checked out of their Leeds hotels on the Monday morning, expecting the game to be over by lunchtime. Botham had other ideas and battered Lillee, Lawson and Alderman for 149 to set up that astonishing victory with Willis taking eight wickets. Another hero of that rearguard action was Graham Dilley. He and Gower stood between us and history now.

Charlie Chatfield put paid to my fears by removing Dilley for 15. In came Bob Taylor for a good stand with Gower. The pair added 27 before Cairns bowled Taylor for 9. Coney then took a brilliant diving catch at slip to send Willis back.

The England lead was 69 and Cowans was the last man. Gower took the initiative and protected his partner skilfully. Coney had a chance to run out Cowans when Gower took a risky single to bring up his century. We didn't have to wait too long for the end. With the new ball, Cairns quickly had Cowans caught bat-pad by Howarth. Still, England had put on 31 for the last wicket. We were left with 101 to win and we knew it wouldn't be easy.

I had to put my personal disappointment to the back of my mind and concentrate on how we would make those tantalising 101 runs. We weren't very adept at chasing 100. In 1980, we lost nine wickets when we beat the West Indies at Dunedin. Only the previous year, we lost four wickets in quick succession against the Aussies. No, it wouldn't be pleasant out there. Nerves would be tested to the limit. We worked out the permutations. If each batsman could manage 10, we were there. If two players got to 30 the game was ours. But could they?

England gave us just the start we wanted with plenty of no-balls, wides and byes. The danger this time was Willis. He came charging in from the same end he used to clean up the Australians, and was no doubt reliving every moment of that mammoth effort. He had Edgar out cheaply, then came storming back in a fierce spell of bowling to dismiss Wright, Howarth and Jeff Crowe. We were 61−4. Was this going to be the collapse of all-time? We hung on until 83 when 'Goose' got rid of Martin Crowe as well. He'd taken all 5 wickets to fall and joined Lillee, Lance Gibbs and Fred Trueman with 300 Test victims. He couldn't have reached the target in a more dramatic manner.

Time seemed to stand still in the dressing room. Cairns and the captain were playing cards; some were watching the play on television and others buried themselves in crosswords, trying to ease the tension. I could imagine all the folks back in New Zealand listening on their radios and chewing their fingernails. By the time I went in, we needed 18 to win with five wickets left. Sometimes 18 can seem a lot of runs! Howarth said to me: 'Make sure of it. No fancy stuff.'

Even so, I'd decided to hit the ball if it was pitched up,

though I doubted I'd get the chance. 'Mantis' and I inched our way nearer to the target. At tea, we were four runs short. It was a formality but I didn't feel very hungry during the break. Willis conceded one run off the first over after tea then tossed the ball to Botham. That was good thinking. Botham had taken 5−1 at Edgbaston in that remarkable series against the Aussies two years back! It was a bit much to expect him to do it again. I overheard Willis say to Botham: 'Come on, golden buttocks, let's see what you can do!' I walked down the pitch and told Coney that the first ball would pitch half way down the wicket. I was right. 'Mantis' pulled it through mid-wicket for four and we had done it!

It had taken fifty-two years to beat England in England. That was our first Test win overseas since we beat Pakistan in Lahore fourteen years before. I had now played in nine victorious New Zealand Tests, more than any other player. It was like a dream. We deserved to win because we had dominated the game and outplayed England in every department. Teamwork was the key factor.

Victory for me was a little flat. It niggled me that I hadn't taken a wicket. I felt I hadn't really contributed, although I scored 75 in the first innings and was there at the end to see the result through. I walked back to the pavilion, up the Headingley steps and hung my helmet on the peg. As I turned around, there was Dad flinging his arms around me.

The dressing room was like a tip . . . champagne, wine and beer all over the floor. Wright had a bowl of ice-cream tipped over his head as he was proclaiming that New Zealand were 'the best team in the world'. The celebrations went on well into the early hours. Most of us came out wearing sunglasses the next day . . . and it wasn't to keep the sun out! Messages arrived from all over New Zealand. Graham Dowling, the secretary of the NZCC went on record as saying: 'The best way to eliminate the patronising attitude the Poms have shown towards New Zealand cricket was to beat them under their own noses. The five-wicket win was like Roger Bannister breaking the four-minute mile!'

Bob Willis was quick to praise and congratulate us, but blasted his team for an inept performance. He'd led by example but had failed to get the response from his

ENGLAND v NEW ZEALAND at Headingley, Leeds

Second Test: July 28, 29, 30 and August 1, 2.

ENGLAND

		First Innings		Second Innings	
1.	C. J. Tavare	c Smith b Coney	69	b Chatfield	23
2.	G. Fowler	c Smith b Chatfield	9	c Smith b Chatfield	19
3.	A. J. Lamb	c M. Crowe b Cairns	58	b Coney	28
4.	D. I. Gower	c Coney b Cairns	9	not out	112
5.	D. W. Randall	c Coney b Cairns	4	c Smith b Chatfield	16
6.	I. T. Botham	c Howarth b Cairns	38	c Howarth b Coney	4
7.	P. H. Edmonds	c Smith b Cairns	8	c Smith b Chatfield	0
8.	R. W. Taylor	not out	10	b Cairns	9
9.	G. R. Dilley	b Cairns	0	c Smith b Chatfield	15
10.	R. G. D. Willis	c J. Crowe b Coney	9	c Coney b Cairns	4
11.	N. G. Cowans	c Bracewell b Cairns	0	c M. Crowe b Cairns	10
	Extras		11		12
	Total		225		252

FALL OF WICKETS:
First innings: 1-18 2-35 3-135 4-175 5-185 6-205 7-205 8-209 9-225
Second innings: 1-39 2-44 3-116 4-126 5-142 6-142 7-190 8-217 9-221.

BOWLERS:

Hadlee	21	9	44	0	26	9	45	0
Chatfield	22	8	67	1	29	5	99	5
Cairns	33.2	14	74	7	24	2	70	3
Coney	12	3	21	2	8	1	30	2
Bracewell	1	0	8	0				

NEW ZEALAND

		First Innings		Second Innings	
1.	J. G. Wright	c Willis b Cowans	93	c Randall b Willis	26
2.	B. A. Edgar	b Willis	84	c Edmonds b Willis	2
3.	G. P. Howarth	run out	13	c Randall b Willis	20
4.	J. J. Crowe	run out	0	b Willis	13
5.	M. D. Crowe	lbw Cowans	37	c Lamb b Willis	1
6.	J. V. Coney	c Gower b Willis	19	not out	10
7.	R. J. Hadlee	b Cowans	75	not out	6
8.	I. D. Smith	c Tavare b Willis	2		
9.	B. L. Cairns	not out	24		
10.	E. J. Chatfield	lbw Willis	0		
11.	J. G. Bracewell	c Dilley b Edmonds	16		
	Extras		14		25
	Total		377	(for 5 wkts)	103

FALL OF WICKETS:
First innings: 1-52 2-168 3-169 4-169 5-218 6-304 7-348 8-351 9-377
Second innings: 1-18 2-42 3-60 4-61 5-83.

Willis	23.3	6	57	4	14	5	35	5
Dilley	17	4	36	0	8	2	16	0
Botham	26	9	81	0	0.1	0	4	0
Cowans	28	8	88	3	5	0	23	0
Edmonds	45	14	101	1				

NEW ZEALAND WON BY 5 WICKETS
Man of Match: B. L. Cairns
Umpires: B. J. Meyer, D. J. Constant.

colleagues. I suppose from his point of view, losing to New Zealand at home was just about the end.

After winning that Test, the stage was set for a close contest in the remaining two Tests at Lords and Trent Bridge. However, we were whitewashed. Our attitude was poor. I got the impression that because we'd done something no other team had done, and the tour was a guaranteed success no matter what followed, we didn't give 100%.

We surrendered to the Poms without a whimper. Losing the series 3-1 after winning the one-day internationals against England was a disgrace. There was very little between the two teams and we should never have lost by that margin. Where was the fight, determination and pride when the chips were down? I didn't see much of it. The younger players thought touring was a great life. Some of them had come into New Zealand cricket at a successful time and seemed to think it was easy. There was a distinct lack of dedication. That's why we were inconsistent when we needed results from individuals who were capable of giving them.

Remarkable though it seems, some players were bitching about the professionals in the team. They didn't think it was right for us to be paid more than the amateurs. I can sympathise with the reason for their grievance, because some of the amateurs made bigger contributions than the pros. What they overlooked was that without professionals, New Zealand cricket would never have reached the heights it had. There was new confidence spreading through our cricket and professionalism was the reason.

I know that the amateurs resented the fact that we'd been offered financial inducements not to play the game abroad. They shouldn't complain. They were paid by their employers while on tour, and still collected their tour allowance, so they weren't too badly off! If players played the game as though their lives depended on it—which ours do—maybe they'd understand the situation better.

Money had reared its head like never before in the camp. I like financial rewards as much as the next man, but I thought there was a little greed creeping into things. A promotions manager was appointed on the England tour and the talk in the dressing room was about how much we could all make out of the game. I think the emphasis was wrong.

Before you can start commanding large sums for promotional work and personal appearances, you have to win. As soon as the lads realised that, they would adopt a more professional outlook, New Zealand would win more Tests, and then they could collect all the fringe benefits. Too many players appear to rely on a select few to do all the work and cover for their own mediocrity. That's an amateurish approach which has no place in modern Test cricket.

On the England tour, if those key players failed—as they were bound to occasionally—the others lost confidence and folded up without a fight. It was doubly frustrating because we had the ability and didn't use it. Time and again we lost wickets in the last hour of the second day—throwing away the advantage we'd won with no chance to get back into the match.

I warned after that series that our attitude had to change when England arrived in New Zealand the following January. We'd have played several Shell Shield games before the Poms got to New Zealand, and would have no excuse for being out of touch. I singled out Gower as the main problem. He'd developed a liking for our bowling. It was essential that we stick to our plan of attack for getting him out. I also warned about the dangers posed by Botham and Lamb, though the one English batsman I overlooked was Derek Randall. He was to have the biggest say of all.

6

Beating The Poms . . . Part II

Expectations were high in New Zealand for the forthcoming visit of Bob Willis and his men. The series was being talked of as the first SERIOUS tour by an England team to the Antipodes. No summer respite this, tagged onto the end of a full tour of Australia. New Zealand would have England's undivided attention for three Tests and three one-day internationals. It was not unrealistic of them to anticipate a home victory. All the indications were that England were going through a transitional period, to put it kindly. Their batting was fragile and the bowling seemed to rely too heavily on an ageing Willis.

If New Zealand were to win their first series against the old enemy, they would certainly need the services of a fit and in-form Richard Hadlee. As 1984 dawned, that began to look distinctly unlikely. Apart from Hadlee's father, few of the New Zealand Council members appreciated what the player had been through. In practice, Hadlee was struggling to find the rhythm which was usually second nature to him. The lessons in positive thought had marked out the path to recovery, but it wasn't going to be an overnight transformation.

I was still sluggish when the First Test came around, though I'd played reasonably well for Canterbury. Mentally I was alright. The desire was there. I wanted to beat the Poms as much as anyone did, but physically, I hadn't had time to get back into proper shape. I looked jaded and weary.

However, when the First Test came along at Wellington's Basin Reserve towards the end of January, we went into a series against England as genuine favourites for the first time in our history. Although England had flattened us in the last two Tests back in the U.K., we had at least broken the spell by winning at Headingley. Now we desperately wanted to go all the way.

We got off to a bad start. At stumps on the first day, you wouldn't have given much for our chances. The Basin Reserve pitch had been pretty well drenched a few days before, but started reasonably dry. England decided to leave out Cowans — a mistake I thought — and include the left arm spinner, Nick Cook.

But it was the irrepressible Botham who ripped us apart. He grabbed the wickets of Wright, Edgar and Howarth with only 56 on the board and finished with 5 — 95. You have to admire the way he rises to the big occasion. I was one of his victims, taken at forward short by Gatting for 24. For someone not in the best nick, I was fairly pleased with that effort, though the team needed something much better. Jeff Crowe was the only one to show any real resistance, scoring 52, but at 219 all out, we were very crestfallen.

Things picked up a bit when England lost 5 wickets for 115. My opening spell didn't feel good, but luckily, Lance Cairns was in superb form and I plucked a couple of smart catches to help England's early collapse. The diving catch to dismiss Gower for 33 was especially pleasing. Botham with his tail up was a discouraging sight. There's nothing an all-rounder likes more than a bunch of wickets under his belt early on. The hard part of the job is out of the way and it means he comes to the wicket relaxed and with his confidence sky-high.

Botham was missed three times early in the innings. He was only in single figures when 'Bootsie' Edgar just failed to get a hand at mid-wicket. Then Martin Snedden made a good attempt to catch a full-blooded drive at mid-off, but the ball went crashing through his hands. The closest was a low one to John Wright at mid-on. He rides his luck well, does Both. I'd be the last one to complain, because I bat in exactly the same way and get my share of good fortune too.

That was all the encouragement he needed. He and Derek Randall pulled the innings out of the fire.

'Arkle', coming in at number seven, played as disciplined an innings as I've seen from him. If only he could do it more often. He was nattering away to himself as usual and the only thing that was going to get him out was his own unpredictability. Apart from playing and missing a few times, he never put a foot wrong in six hours and seven minutes. That was some effort! Randall was to be a real problem all series. He almost pipped me to Man of the Series and was a world class performer throughout the tour.

You wouldn't have put any money on me for Man of the Series at Wellington! I had Derek out eventually, but 2 – 97 was a disappointing show. With England getting to 463 thanks to Botham's 138 and Derek's 164, we thought we were in for a hammering. My earlier warning about New Zealand having to sharpen their attitude seemed to have fallen on deaf ears. That is, until Jeremy Coney joined Martin Crowe in our second innings.

I guess the average New Zealand spectator must have been expecting the innings to fold after Geoff Howarth was unluckily run out and Botham had Jeff Crowe lbw for 3. Kiwi supporters have been bred on failure and have a natural tendency to be pessimistic. What they witnessed next was an unbelievable innings from Coney, or 'Mantis' as we call him. Neither he nor Martin had ever scored a Test century. In fact it was seven years since 'Mantis' had scored a century at all in first class cricket! What a time they picked to break their personal bests.

Both scored maiden Test centuries and Coney with 174 not out went on to set a New Zealand record against England at home. I gather the previous best was set by Trish McKelvey, the New Zealand captain playing in a women's Test against England at the same ground! There were incredible scenes in our dressing room. We logged every ball, every over and every run as Crowe and Coney edged us nearer and nearer to safety. We were eventually bowled out for 537 and forced a draw. It gave us a great deal of confidence because, despite their recent record, England were still a very good and professional side, well capable

ENGLAND v NEW ZEALAND
First Test
January 20, 21, 22, 23, 24 — Wellington

NEW ZEALAND

		First Innings		Second Innings	
1.	J. G. Wright	c Cook b Botham	17	c Foster b Cook	35
2.	B. A. Edgar	c Taylor b Botham	9	c Taylor b Willis	30
3.	G. P. Howarth	c Gower b Botham	15	run out	34
4.	M. D. Crowe	b Willis	13	c Botham b Gatting	100
5.	J. J. Crowe	c Taylor b Foster	52	lbw b Botham	3
6.	J. V. Coney	c Gower b Cook	27	not out	174
7.	R. J. Hadlee	c Gatting b Botham	24	c Lamb b Foster	18
8.	M. C. Snedden	c Taylor b Willis	11	c Taylor b Foster	16
9.	I. D. S. Smith	lbw b Botham	24	b Cook	29
10.	B. L. Cairns	c Gatting b Willis	3	c sub (Fowler) b Willis	64
11.	E. J. Chatfield	not out	4	b Cook	0
	Extras		20		34
	Total		219		537

FALL OF WICKETS:
First innings: 1-34 2-39 3-56 4-71 5-114 6-160 7-174 8-200 9-208
Second innings: 1-62 2-79 3-153 4-165 5-279 6-302 7-334 8-402 9-520.

BOWLERS:

Willis	19	7	37	3	37	8	102	2
Botham	27.4	8	59	5	36	6	137	1
Foster	24	9	60	1	37	12	91	2
Cook	23	1	43	1	66.3	26	153	3
Gatting					8	4	14	1
Smith					3	1	6	0

ENGLAND

		First Innings		Second Innings	
1.	C. J. Tavare	b Cairns	9	not out	36
2.	C. L. Smith	c Hadlee b Cairns	27	not out	30
3.	D. I. Gower	c Hadlee b Cairns	33		
4.	A. J. Lamb	c M. Crowe b Cairns	13		
5.	M. W. Gatting	lbw b Cairns	19		
6.	I. T. Botham	c J. Crowe b Cairns	138		
7.	D. W. Randall	c M. Crowe b Hadlee	164		
8.	R. W. Taylor	run out	14		
9.	N. G. B. Cook	c Smith b Cairns	7		
10.	N. A. Foster	c Howarth b Hadlee	10		
11.	R. G. D. Willis	not out	5		
	Extras		24		3
	Total		463	(for no wkts)	69

FALL OF WICKETS:
First innings: 1-41 2-51 3-84 4-92 5-115 6-347 7-372 8-386 9-426

BOWLERS:

Hadlee	31.5	6	97	2			
Snedden	21	3	101	0	7	2	28	0
Cairns	45	10	143	7			
Chatfield	28	6	68	0	5	0	24	0
M. Crowe	3	0	20	0	6	1	11	0
Coney	4	1	10	0			
Edgar					3	1	3	0
J. Crowe					1	1	0	0

MATCH DRAWN
Man of the Match: I. T. Botham
Umpires: F. R. Goodall, S. J. Woodward

---

of winning. The result at Wellington, and the way it was achieved made us realise that we were more than capable of winning as well. If we could get into a strong position in the Second Test, we fancied our chances.

I'd been having a bit of a niggle in my side and was still below par. The Board was looking ahead to the Sri Lanka series which was coming up immediately after the England tour. Frankly, the thought of going to a tropical country in my frail condition was a big worry.

I'd not been there before but had heard stories about the heat and humidity, about food problems and questionable hotels, that sort of thing. In view of what I'd just experienced, I didn't think I was capable of getting through the tour and doing myself and my country justice. Shortly before the First Test finished, I told our chairman, Bob Vance that I was unlikely to be available. The Board said they'd give me another ten days to think about it. I agreed for their sake, but couldn't see much hope.

That all changed in the sensational Second Test. It was a breakthrough not only for New Zealand cricket, but for me personally. Much of the glory has been taken away from the most convincing Test victory in our entire history. The pitch has been blamed for the match finishing in twelve hours one minute, and for England suffering their biggest humiliation since 1895. Bob Willis said that the three Tests in which New Zealand had beaten England — Wellington in 1978 (under Geoff Boycott), Headingley in 1983 and now Christchurch in 1984, were all played on sub-standard

63

wickets. What he forgot to mention was that when they last beat us at Lords in the 1983 tour, the wicket was probably worse than Lancaster Park!

Let's be perfectly honest, Lancaster Park wasn't up to Test match standard. In fact, the Test was very nearly switched to Napier because of it. There'd been a couple of first-class matches on it before the Test and the results weren't that good—a lot of inconsistency in the bounce, with the ball alternately rearing off a length then scudding along the ground. The trouble with pitches like Lancaster Park is that they're dual-purpose. All winter long, rugby is played there and in a couple of months at the end of the rugby season, the groundsman has to turn a bog into a first-class pitch for cricket. He should get credit for making something out of nothing every year.

The truth of the matter is that England allowed themselves to be 'psyched out' before they started. Conditions were the same for both sides and New Zealand adapted to them better. Winning the toss was vital, but I dare say Bob Willis would have put us in first. Geoff Howarth confounded the critics by choosing to bat.

He had confidence in his batsmen to overcome the conditions, although he also figured that if the pitch was as devilish as people were making out, batting last would be best avoided.

There was no question that the ball dominated the bat. After the first few overs, Willis looked a real menace. He sat Wright and Edgar on their rumps with balls that rose steeply off a length. For a while, life out in the middle looked terrifying.

Botham didn't make the best use of it. Two balls in his first over were bowled more or less straight at the slips! When he did get on target, Wright pulled him fiercely to the boundary. It seemed to me that Botham was in one of those carefree moods. It was to prove England's undoing.

The pitch settled down quite quickly, and we had in mind a total of 250-280. The occasional ball kept low, but Willis's were the only two fliers of the morning session. England were pretty pleased with their efforts. We'd lost our first four batsmen for 87 at lunch and Tony Pigott had collected his maiden Test wicket, making one 'stop' on Edgar who spooned it to Randall. Pigott had been recruited from Wellington where he was playing in the Trophy, because of injuries to Graham Dilley and Neil Foster. He was due to be married on the Monday of the Test and had to postpone the ceremony. As it turned out, he needn't have bothered!

Jeff Crowe and Coney made all the fuss about the wicket look exaggerated when they each got into the 40's playing sensibly and well. Cowans was the pick of the England bowlers, yet when I came in to bat at number seven, he bowled only three balls at me. I never saw him again I'm glad to say. For a couple of hours either side of tea, he didn't get used. Willis brought Botham back into the attack, though I imagine Botham more or less asked to have a go at me. The rivalry between us was intense. It carried over after the cricket when we gave each other a wide berth. After an article I wrote in one of our local papers, I heard he was 'gunning for me'.

He didn't show it in that game. Pigott and Botham bowled much too short and wide and gave me all the room I needed to take the attack to them. They knew I was a strokemaker who liked to get on with it, yet they gave me all the encouragement I wanted! In eighty-one deliveries and less than two hours, I made more runs than the entire England team could manage in either innings. It changed the whole course of the match. Coney and I put on some very quick runs — 66 in 62 minutes for the sixth wicket.

I went for everything and invented some shots as I went along. There were plenty of fielders in so I whacked a lot of balls away over mid-wicket. Many of my shots were in the air, but they were safe. The bowling also gave me ample opportunity to play my favourite front-foot drives. One of them, I remember, bisected two men at long-off! I was enjoying every minute and couldn't understand why England insisted on trying to bounce us out or bowl us out. It was a big mistake with me playing that sort of innings. They should have bowled wicket to wicket and tried to contain me. I hit Botham for four fours in an over and took 40 from Pigott's 6 overs after tea. I'd never felt better.

When tea came we were 203 — 5 and our estimate of 250

65

ENGLAND v NEW ZEALAND

Second Test
February 3, 4, 5, – Christchurch

NEW ZEALAND
First Innings

1.	J. G. Wright	c Taylor b Cowans	25
2.	B. A. Edgar	c Randall b Pigott	1
3.	*G. P. Howarth	b Cowans	9
4.	M. D. Crowe	c Tavare b Botham	19
5.	J. J. Crowe	lbw b Cowans	47
6.	J. V. Coney	c Botham b Pigott	41
7.	R. J. Hadlee	c Taylor b Willis	99
8.	† I. D. S. Smith	not out	32
9.	B. L. Cairns	c Taylor b Willis	2
10.	S. L. Boock	c Taylor b Willis	5
11.	E. J. Chatfield	lbw b Willis	0
	Extras		27
	Total		307

FALL OF WICKETS:
First innings: 1-30 2-42 3-53 4-87 5-137 6-203 7-281 8-291 9-301

BOWLERS:

Willis	22.1	5	51	4
Botham	17	1	88	1
Pigott	17	7	75	2
Cowans	14	2	52	3
Gatting	2	0	14	0

ENGLAND
First Innings   **Second Innings**

		First Innings		Second Innings	
1.	G. Fowler	b Boock	4	c Howarth b Boock	10
2.	C. J. Tavare	c J. Crowe b Hadlee	3	c Smith b Hadlee	6
3.	D. I. Gower	lbw b Hadlee	2	c Cairns b Hadlee	8
4.	A. J. Lamb	c Smith b Chatfield	11	c Coney b Chatfield	9
5.	D. W. Randall	c Coney b Hadlee	0	c Cairns b Hadlee	25
6.	I. T. Botham	c Chatfield b Cairns	18	c M. Crowe b Boock	0
7.	M. W. Gatting	not out	19	c Hadlee b Boock	0
8.	† R. W. Taylor	c J. Crowe b Cairns	2	run out	15
9.	A. C. S. Pigott	lbw b Cairns	4	not out	8
10.	* R. G. D. Willis	b Chatfield	6	c Howarth b Hadlee	0
11.	N. G. Cowans	c Coney b Chatfield	4	c Smith b Hadlee	7
	Extras		9		5
	Total		82		93

FALL OF WICKETS:
First innings: 1-7 2-9 3-10 4-10 5-41 6-41 7-47 8-58 9-72
Second innings: 1-15 2-23 3-25 4-31 5-31 6-33 7-72 8-76 9-80

BOWLERS:

Hadlee	17	9	16	3	17.5	6	28	5
Cairns	19	5	35	3	9	3	21	0
Boock	6	3	12	1	13	3	25	3
Chatfield	8.2	3	10	3	11	1	14	1

NEW ZEALAND WON BY AN INNINGS AND 132 RUNS
Man of the Match: R. J. Hadlee
Umpires: F. R. Goodall, S. J. Woodward

plus was well within reach. Soon after the break, I lost Coney. Next man in was Ian Smith who'd been under a lot of pressure from Warren Lees for his wicket-keeping place. Lees' batting record was much better than Smith's but he knuckled down well and bettered his personal best. He helped me to add a further 78 runs. There was still no sign of Cowans, so I just carried on swinging the bat. Eventually, I went for one shot too many on 99, flicking at a short ball from Willis and giving Bob Taylor a catch behind. I could have left it alone, but it's not my style.

I think other people were more disappointed about me missing the century than I was. In the circumstances, I reckon that 99 was worth 150. How could I be disappointed in that? Thanks to Ian Smith with his 32 not out, we stretched the score to 307 — highly satisfactory. The day ended with another bonus when Stephen Boock came on with his left-arm spin for the last over and bowled Fowler with his first ball in Test cricket for nearly four years.

Steady overnight rain lasted well into the second day. It was very frustrating. We were longing to get after the England batsmen but all we could do was play cards into the afternoon. At about 4.30 p.m., the groundstaff had the pitch ready for play to resume. England were soon wishing they hadn't.

Our bowlers learned from Botham and Pigott's mistakes. All we needed to do was bowl line and length and commit the batsmen to playing the ball. We did just that for 100 overs and had England out twice in double figures. On the second day, they only had an hour and a half's batting, but succeeded in producing one of the most sensational Test collapses. They'd sunk to 53 — 7 by stumps, with Cairns, Chatfield and myself all creating havoc.

I had Chris Tavare early with a fast leg-cutter which he

edged to Jeff Crowe at first slip. That was an important wicket. Tavare is capable of staying around for hours just prodding and blocking. Next, to my astonishment, Gower shouldered arms to a low straight one and was out leg-before. Gower didn't seem to know where his stumps were. None of the England batsmen appeared to have an ounce of confidence. Two balls after Gower had gone, Randall poked at another cutter to give Coney the catch at second slip. That was 10−4. Poor Derek was so bemused by it all, he had to be pointed in the direction of the pavilion!

The pitch was ideally suited to Ewen Chatfield, but as yet, he hadn't had a chance to use it. After my 3−13 burst, he got it. Allan Lamb obliged by snicking a catch behind. Botham had already departed, caught in the deep by Chatfield going after a slow one from Cairns. We predicted an England total of 75 and were only seven runs out. The next morning, Cairns and Chatfield finished off the tail. England had been shot out for 82 and the three pacemen had taken three wickets apiece. At least England did slightly better than Geoff Boycott's team at Wellington which was bowled out for 64.

I saved my best bowling for the second innings. Tavare edged one to Ian Smith behind the wicket then Gower fell victim to the off-stump attack, chipping a catch to Cairns at third slip. Once again, Fowler fell to Boock, giving a bat-pad catch to Howarth at silly point. If England had any thoughts of a fightback, Boock removed them in one over. Gatting tried to drive, only to present me with a catch at slip, and next ball, Botham pushed forward to be well taken by Martin Crowe at short leg. Botham sauntered back with a wide grin on his face.

At the other end, Lamb edged Chatfield wide of Coney who somehow held onto the catch and it was almost over at 33−6. Randall and Taylor put up some good resistance, but after Taylor was run out by another excellent piece of fielding by Edgar, I made one bounce a bit higher to Randall who got a thick edge to Cairns in the gully. Derek had made 25 and was going very well at that stage. It was the only responsible England innings of the match. Then I wrapped up the tail, removing Willis and Cowans to finish with 5−28 and a match analysis of 8−44, England had totalled 93 and we had beaten them by an innings and 132 runs.

Throughout the game, only three or four balls lifted awkwardly, but that was enough to make the Englishmen think there was dynamite in every delivery. Their performance was inept. They didn't treat each ball on its merits. Instead, they were tentative and sparred at the bowling, more often than not nicking it to the slips area. Twelve of the twenty dismissals were caught behind or in the slips and two bat-pad catches were taken from half-hearted push shots.

We took some magnificent catches . . . 95% of the chances offered were accepted. It's funny that Willis criticised his bowlers for giving away runs, but never said a word about his batsmen. He preferred to blame the pitch instead. That was unfair because it took a lot of the credit away from our performance. Bowling out a team like that for 82 in the first innings and 93 in the second has got to be an outstanding effort. Willis' batsmen simply weren't prepared to graft — they gave the game away.

We bowled four attempted bouncers at them, they bowled more than thirty at us. They allowed me to hit eighteen boundaries in my 99, but we allowed them only fourteen boundaries in two completed innings. I believe that, had we played any other side in similar circumstances, we would have whipped them. We sensed victory and followed it through.

This success turned everything around for me. I'd played a major part in the victory which was important in restoring my confidence. In the First Test I didn't feel I was really doing the team an awful lot of good and certainly lacked match fitness. My position as the number one was threatened. After Christchurch, I was back on top and loving it. The atmosphere had been just right with the home crowd backing me. I won the 'Man of the Match' award and my attitude was improving with each day.

I turned my mind to the question of Sri Lanka again. There were only a few days before I had to make my decision known to the Board. Instead of deciding there and then, I waited until the Third Test just to see if I really was back to my best.

At this point, I feel I must say a few words in defence of Russ Wylie, the groundsman at Lancaster Park which was denied a Test match for the home series against Pakistan in 1984-5. I was surprised and disappointed to hear that decision, taken because of the two-day win over England a year earlier. The New Zealand Cricket Council was being very premature. Its verdict showed a complete lack of confidence in the groundsman to produce good pitches for the coming season. It appears that the NZCC has removed the incentive for him to get the pitches right. It could have waited until December. If Lancaster Park wasn't up to standard by then, it wouldn't have been too late to switch to Dunedin or Napier.

It is right to say that the Christchurch pitch was not Test match standard last season, but it produced a result—a win for New Zealand which enabled us to take the series. The venues for Pakistan: Auckland, Wellington and Dunedin are all likely to produce draws. I'm sure the public will be denied a true spectacle.

I have found wicket-taking at Eden Park, Auckland very difficult (as most bowlers have); the Basin Reserve at Wellington hasn't been as kind to me as it was earlier in my career, and Carisbrook, Dunedin is very much an unknown quantity. I've only played two first class matches there, one of them a Test match when I took eleven wickets against the West Indies on a slow wicket with no bounce.

In contrast, I've got wickets and runs at Lancaster Park over the years and Russ Wylie has produced some excellent Test pitches. The pitch produced by Cyril Barnes for the West Indian series in 1980 was good too; two years later, the Aussies beat us on another good pitch; we beat Sri Lanka in 1983 and England in 1984. Now, after one controversial pitch, Lancaster Park and the people of Christchurch were being severely punished. Without trying to blow my own trumpet too much, the fact is that when New Zealand win Tests, I usually get wickets. Lancaster Park has produced a few for me, and allowed New Zealand to win three Tests in my time. Even when we have lost or drawn, I've got my share.

I shall certainly miss playing there against Pakistan. My

wicket tally could be well down on my budget for the series. Eden Park has only allowed me two to three wickets a Test, the Basin Reserve four and Lancaster Park eight-plus in recent times.

In England on the 1983 tour, the pitches at Lords and Headingley came in for heavy criticism. Lords was dangerous while Headingley suited our seamers but was inconsistent in bounce. The Lancaster Park pitch was no worse, and probably better than those two. Both English pitches have had bad reports for some years, but both staged Tests when England played the West Indies in 1984. They've been reprieved, but Lancaster Park gets the chop.

What the NZCC perhaps didn't appreciate was how much the English media and players enjoyed the decision to ban it as a Test venue. It means, in their eyes, that our administrators have admitted that it cost England the series. It means that the New Zealand team takes little or no credit for winning.

I went through the third and final Test at Auckland feeling good. I felt it was the best I've done with the ball for a long time, getting through the work nicely and feeling fitter all the time. The more I played, the more rhythmical and co-ordinated I became.

We arrived at Eden Park knowing exactly what we had to do. One up and one to play called for an easy pitch, some luck with the toss and plenty of dedicated batting if we were to achieve our cherished ambition of a series win over England. In the event, we got all three. Our unashamed strategy was not to lose. Not many results have been achieved at Eden Park. The last time we played England in a six-day Test in 1978, only three innings were completed. That says it all. It's a docile pitch, a bit like Edgbaston — no encouragement for the bowlers, a dream for the batsmen. It's a funny ground too. The angle of the wicket means that two of the boundaries are short, another minus point for the bowler. As you run in to bowl, the earth is hollow-sounding. You hear the thud-thud-thud of your feet which is a bit distracting!

Geoff Howarth's first task was to win the toss then bat for as long as possible. Our first innings lasted almost as long

71

ENGLAND v NEW ZEALAND
Third Test
February 10, 11, 12, 14, 15 — Auckland

NEW ZEALAND

		First Innings		**Second Innings**	
1.	J. G. Wright	b Willis	130	not out	11
2.	B. A. Edgar	lbw b Willis	0	not out	0
3.	*G. P. Howarth	c Randall b Cowans	35		
4.	M. D. Crowe	c Botham b Willis	16		
5.	J. J. Crowe	b Marks	128		
6.	J. V. Coney	b Cowans	9		
7.	R. J. Hadlee	b Marks	3		
8.	† I. D. S. Smith	not out	113		
9.	B. L. Cairns	c Cowans b Foster	28		
10.	S. L. Boock	lbw b Marks	2		
11.	E. J. Chatfield	not out	6		
	Extras (lb19, nb7)		26	(nb4, lb1)	5
	Total for 9 wkts declared		**496**	**Total for no wickets**	**16**

FALL OF WICKETS:
First innings: 1-3 2-74 3-111 4-265 5-293 6-302 7-385 8-451 9-461

BOWLERS:

Willis	34	7	109	3	3	1	7	0
Botham	29	10	70	0				
Cowans	36	11	98	2	2	1	4	0
Foster	30	8	78	1				
Marks	40.2	9	115	3				

ENGLAND
First Innings

1.	G. Fowler	c Smith b Hadlee	0
2.	C. L. Smith	c Smith b Cairns	91
3.	D. I. Gower	b Boock	26
4.	A. J. Lamb	lbw b Cairns	49
5.	D. W. Randall	c Wright b Chatfield	104
6.	† R. W. Taylor	st Smith b Boock	23
7.	I. T. Botham	run out	70
8.	V. J. Marks	c Smith b Chatfield	6
9.	N. A. Foster	not out	18
10.	* R. G. Willis	c Smith b Hadlee	3
11.	N. G. Cowans	c Cairns b Boock	21
	Extras (b7, lb13, nb8)		28
	Total		**439**

FALL OF WICKETS:
First innings: 1-0 2-48 3-143 4-234 5-284 6-371 7-387 8-391 9-396

BOWLERS:

Hadlee	43	12	91	2
Cairns	40	19	52	2

Boock	61.3	28	103	3
Chatfield	46	23	72	2
M. Crowe	17	5	62	0
Coney	13	8	13	0
Howarth	7	2	18	0

MATCH DRAWN
NEW ZEALAND WON SERIES 1-0
Man of the Match: I. D. S. Smith
Umpires: F. R. Goodall, S. J. Woodward

as the entire Second Test! Not a tremendous treat for the spectators perhaps, but I think they were happy enough to see England beaten in a series for the first time. These things are important to New Zealanders. England didn't get a look-in.

In the five days, only nineteen wickets fell for 952 runs. The pitch was flat and brown and tailor-made for batting. No complaints from Bob Willis this time, though, in all fairness, pitches like that don't do an awful lot for the game. You could say that Lancaster Park, for all its defects, at least provides some excitement.

Willis gave us an early scare when he came around the wicket to Bruce Edgar and bowled him with the total on 3. There weren't too many worries after that. Centuries by Wright, Jeff Crowe and a maiden hundred for Ian Smith saw us to a score of 496−6 declared.

That was our highest-ever total at Eden Park and the first time three home players had topped a hundred in a home Test. For the handful of English supporters dotted around the ground, it must have been an enormous yawn, but for our supporters, tired of sitting through long and tedious Test innings by the opposition, it was a just reward. All three centurions played lovely shots all around the wicket.

We'd no sooner finished congratulating Ian on his first test hundred than we were congratulating him again on taking the catch to dismiss Fowler for a duck when England went in. I was the bowler, and was surprised to see Fowler groping for the first ball he received. His last three innings had been a nightmare. Gower's hadn't been much better. He missed one from Boock which hit his off stump and England were

73

54—2 at stumps on the third day. A curious thing occurred to me as the last few balls were bowled. The men at the crease were Lamb and Chris Smith. Not a true Englishman in sight! Only nine more like that, and we could be playing South Africa!

Smith went on to complete an eight-hour 91 and Randall compiled another century. It was a fruitless exercise that only statisticians could have enjoyed apart from us.

Just before the end of the Test, I had a meeting with the Council to decide once and for all whether I was going to Sri Lanka. I told them I would be available, but that I'd be doubtful for the trip to Pakistan eight months later. I thought New Zealand's commitment was too great. The Pakistan tour was scheduled for November/December, then Pakistan would play in New Zealand in the New Year. After that it would be off to Australia for the mini-World Cup, then, in March off for a tour of the West Indies before flying back to England again in April.

I warned them what had happened to me through overdoing things, and stressed that I had to have a break sometime. They didn't like the thought of my pulling out of the Pakistan trip, but understood my point of view.

England gained some revenge by winning the Rothmans' one-day international series 2-1. One of their victories was at the famous Lancaster Park! I was delighted to win 'Man of the Series' for the one-dayers and the Test matches. My prize was a Toyota car which we sold for 16,000 dollars and distributed among the team. I ended up with a wheel for my contribution to the series, but it didn't worry me too much. The pride of winning the title was more important than the money.

I was glad when the England series was over. It had been a testing time for me. Once you've had a breakdown, you're in unknown territory and you're very wary about not overtaxing your mind and body again. I'd judged it just about right, but I was tired and looking forward to a few days rest before Sri Lanka.

The England series was a very happy one. Relations with Bob Willis and the boys were excellent, despite the complaints over the Lancaster Park pitch. I was delighted to see our approach to Test cricket hardened up. We'd been much more determined than usual throughout the series — never prepared to give England an inch. I sincerely hope we see more of it.

While the series was in progress, there was no hint of anything controversial. It was only when we were playing in Sri Lanka that we got to hear about the drug allegations surrounding the English players. Several English reporters flew to Sri Lanka to get our views, but we were told to say nothing. We had no evidence, and the issue was nothing to do with us.

I will say that there were some inconsistencies in the reports. A lot of the allegations seemed to stem from a party thrown by Jeff Crowe. According to the stories, this was some great eve-of-the-series shindig. That is wrong. The party was right at the end of the series, when the last of the one-day internationals had been played. I was there and certainly saw no evidence of drugs. Taking cannabis is very much frowned upon in New Zealand, as it is in England. I don't imagine it would be too easy to get hold of.

7

Stop The Treadmill—
I Want To Get Off!

From television gantries, high above the big urban grounds like Trent Bridge and The Oval, events on the green oasis below take on a curious appearance. While the rest of the city bustles about its noisy, smoky business, there, cocooned from the harsh world of trade and commerce, thirteen men try to engage the interest of a few old boys sucking their pipes and remembering summers that will never return. Viewed dispassionately, county cricket is a bizarre ritual which seems to make no commercial sense whatever. Wasn't it Archbishop Temple who remarked that he'd always looked upon cricket as organised loafing? We know the reality is different. In England especially, the game is much harder than an outsider could imagine. Well paid at the top, yes, but gruelling. Richard Hadlee again:

Cricket to me is a job, not a sport. Enjoyment rarely comes into it. Some mornings when I wake up and think about the twenty-five overs I've got to bowl, I'd just as soon roll over in bed and forget it. At times like that I feel like getting out of the game and becoming an accountant—a nice, comfortable office job with regular hours and no exertion! Somehow you overcome those moments by reminding yourself that it's your job and you've damned well got to get out there and perform.

Normally, I arrive at the ground at 9.30 a.m. and go through the time-honoured business of getting changed into tracksuit, doing a lap or two of the ground, a few exercises, a bit of fielding practice then returning to the pavilion for a cup of tea and a look at the papers while we wait to see whether we're batting or bowling. Fitness is no great problem. I have no trouble with putting on weight so I don't need to train too heavily. Footballers always tell me how much work they have to do but they only play twice a week at the most. We never stop!

Trevor Tunnicliffe used to be in charge of training. We preferred to call him Adolf! He worked us till we were sick. Now the club has a policy of leaving fitness to the individual. That suits me. I don't want to be running five miles a day at my stage of life. I'm so lightly built anyway that I'd probably disappear altogether if I burned off any more energy!

Whichever way you look at it, the county circuit is a treadmill. I can't complain too much because it's my decision to play so I must accept the ups and downs. The routine is the same every day. Nothing ever changes. I've often asked myself what I'm doing flogging my tired body around the country, but I suppose it's the same in any job.

The drudgery comes from seven days cricket on the trot, sometimes fourteen or fifteen without a break. They're long days too, especially when the 117 over rule was in force. We're forever driving or being driven up and down the country, staying in different hotels, strange beds, picking up a quick meal somewhere then trailing back home for a couple of days with the family before the cycle starts again. There's no other country where we'd spend so much time on the road. Anywhere else, we'd fly from match to match. People in New Zealand often ask me what I think of places like London, Brighton, Cheltenham, Harrogate, etc., and I have to explain that I never see them. All I see of England in my five months a year is a series of cricket grounds, hotels, motorways, my home in Nottingham and the back garden. Very often we're travelling in the dark so we don't even see that much.

There has to be county cricket to produce players for Test teams, but the format is wrong. There is just too much cricket. Demands on players are getting ridiculous. Internationals have to perform for ten or eleven months of the year and before long, I'm afraid, something will have to give. You may find more players jumping off the merry-go-round like Botham and I have. Not only do we get physically exhausted, but we lose our appetite for the game and grow as stale as old bread by the end of a summer. It's small wonder England has problems finding new talent. The players must get worn down by the schedule.

The Cricketer's Association recommended not so long ago that the number of county games be reduced from twenty-two to twenty, but what happened? The Test and County Cricket Board went and INCREASED the fixture list to twenty-four. Crazy! What I'd like to see is a complete break from cricket half way through the season. A midsummer holiday if you like. Players could get away with their families, recover from niggling injuries and recharge their batteries.

Apart from the therapeutic value, it might also help to root out the mediocrity that's crept into the English game. With fewer games, the 'If I fail today, there's always tomorrow' brigade wouldn't get away with it. They'd be expected to achieve more over a shorter period. If they didn't come up to scratch, there'd be nowhere for them to hide. I know there'll be plenty of knockers who say you can't stop in the middle of summer because the sunny period in England is so short. What I'm saying is that if we can't stop that treadmill, English cricket will drive itself into the ground.

The number of games should be reduced from twenty-four to sixteen. Each match would last for three to four days and each county would play the other once only. The present system is unjust. You can draw a top team or a bottom one twice in the season. How can the championship be fair on that basis? The Natwest and the Benson and Hedges could continue, but with only one championship match a week, perhaps on a Monday, Tuesday and Wednesday, we'd all get the chance of 2 days a week off. On Saturdays why not introduce another one-day competition but make it a 50-over contest with no short run ups?

At the moment, Sundays are the toughest days of the week. I don't know many players who enjoy John Player League. It's a money-earner for the game, but it's not a barrel of fun for the players. We're mentally and physically involved each minute of the day — fielding for forty overs, bowling eight, then chasing runs against the over-rate. It's exhausting. I shouldn't like to be captain on Sundays — my head would be spinning.

Commercialism has taken such a grip on the game that the merry-go-round seems to be going faster and faster. It's easy to see why it's happened. In my country, the Board has just cottoned on to the fact that cricket is big business. Now that New Zealand are on the crest of a wave, a whole new world has opened up. The national team is in demand almost as much as the West Indies, Australia and England. While the going's good, there's a temptation to be greedy. If there's the slightest chance of squeezing in an extra tour or one-day tournament, we squeeze it in. Most Test players want to dip their bread and good luck to them. For the select few expected to be the matchwinners, it's increasingly difficult to keep producing the goods on a nominated day at a certain event.

Psychologically, the hardest cricket to play is club cricket in New Zealand. Not wishing to be unkind, the opposition sometimes isn't up to much and the pitches, to say the least, are varied. The other lads are dying to have a go at me because of my reputation and if I don't score fifty or take five wickets, I get all the stick from the press. Reporters usually take a negative line. It would be 'Hadlee fails' rather than: 'So and so batted well for his hundred'.

I've had one or two very embarrassing moments. For instance, Clive and I played in a sort of pro-am club match one day at Cleethorpes. The idea was that each side was allowed one pro — Clive and myself — but we weren't allowed to bowl. It was a twenty-over game so clearly we were expected to put on a bit of an exhibition. The two openers in my side were stubborn Yorkshiremen who seemed to have taken a page out of Boycott's book. They wouldn't get out and neither would they push the score along very fast. After 13 overs, the pair were still there and my captain promoted me to next man in because there were only 7 overs left.

Eventually one of them got out and I went in with the spectators no doubt expecting a riot of runs. They were soon disillusioned. The third or fourth ball I tried to blitz over midwicket and was bowled for 0! The umpire should have quickly called a no-ball, but for some reason he wouldn't. I had no choice but to retrace my steps to the pavilion. To make up for it, they had to change the rules and allow me to bowl.

Bowling against lesser opposition I always find difficult. To qualify for the Benson and Hedges we had to take at least eight wickets against the Minor Counties at Trent Bridge in May. I bowled eleven overs, five maidens and took 1 — 8. They couldn't actually lay bat on ball. The lads in the slips were having kittens each time the batsmen played and missed.

Clive came on to bowl and the same thing happened. They couldn't get near the ball. It suddenly dawned on him that to get wickets, he had to bowl rubbish. He tossed up a few slow bouncers and half-volleys and sure enough, the guys were holing out to mid-wicket or cover-point. I couldn't believe it. I'd bowled my heart out for nothing and there was the captain picking up the wickets. Finally, with a solitary man posted on the leg side, Clive bowled another soft one. The batsman walloped it — straight down mid-wicket's throat! I just collapsed with laughter. If that was how to take wickets, what was cricket all about?

Strange as it may seem, Test cricket comes more easily to me even though the pressure's much greater. I'm playing in an arena and an atmosphere to which I'm more accustomed. The pitches are better and so is the opposition. In addition, I know that whatever I do will be reported nationwide, if not worldwide, and seen by millions on television. It gives me an incentive to be at my best and improve my international rating.

I'm an impatient bloke. Sitting around in dressing rooms for hours on end bores me to tears. I'm not a great watcher of cricket. Perhaps the odd over or two, then I'll bury myself in a crossword or write one of my newspaper articles, or, better still, snatch a quick kip.

Rainy days can be terrible. Out come the cards and the books. When you think about it, the time wasted in the dressing room is enormous if you add it up over the course of a season. Sometimes you welcome the rain, especially if nothing's at stake and the match is going nowhere. We were hardly ever in that position last summer. Rain was a positive enemy. It could stop me reaching my goal.

The road to the double had reached match number nine, Gloucestershire at Trent Bridge . . . and a crisis looming on the batting front.

It was 16th June and the visitors had no answer to Hadlee when Rice put them in. As he'd predicted in his budget, Gloucestershire would provide rich pickings. In fifteen and a half overs, Hadlee took 7—35. Four of the victims were caught by Bruce French behind the wicket and the young Notts keeper was well on his way to becoming wicket-keeper of the year.

Hadlee claimed four more wickets in the second innings to take him within three of his target of five wickets per game. The runs were a big worry. A century from John Birch and seventies from Broad and Robinson saw Notts to a total of 398—7 declared and an innings win. Once more, Hadlee managed one visit to the crease and could score only 17 before being caught by Paul Romaines off the bowling of Gary Sainsbury.

Worse was in store at Grace Road in the drawn game with Leicestershire. Bad light and rain interrupted the game with the result that both teams only had one full innings each. Notts reached one of their highest scores of the season, 404 with Robinson in the middle of a purple patch. He scored 171 and 85 not out in the abortive second innings and followed it with 169 and 45 in the next fixture against Yorkshire. How Hadlee could have done with a boost of that nature. Andy Roberts had him caught by Nick Cook for 9.

Robinson's form, and two big scores from Randall when Yorkshire arrived at Trent Bridge spelled more disappointment in the double chase.

Batting first, Notts made 390—5 declared. Yorkshire replied with 341 (Bairstow 91) and Rice declared a second time at 259—5. The upshot was that Hadlee didn't pick up his bat!

Coming up to the halfway stage, the runs had reached 366. It looked a bit doubtful then. Only thirteen games to go and

633 runs required. I was beginning to get obsessional, worrying about the weather and the risk of injury. On top of that, we were going so well that the chance of two innings a game seemed very remote. What I needed was another century somewhere. Now I had started this thing and made my aims public, I had to see it through and get it out of my system.

On the other hand, it was vital that I didn't put the double ahead of the team's objectives. I couldn't concentrate on playing for myself. Although we'd virtually lost Mike Hendrick with injury for the season, we were right up there at the top with a great chance of winning the title. Having already beaten Essex, we had a psychological advantage over them and Leicestershire seemed to have peaked.

Rice went through the Leicester fixture card working out how many games he thought they'd win. His conclusion was that they would struggle from now on, and he was perfectly right.

Hadlee didn't get his century in the Sussex match which marked the half way point of the season. However, he did collect 83 runs in two innings to bring himself right back into the picture. He scored 16 first time and 67 in no time at all in the second innings. Notts won by 142 runs and now stood 4 points behind Leicestershire with a game in hand. They had not, as yet, been top of the table.

His bowling was ticking over nicely. Four wickets in each innings ripped the heart out of the Sussex batting. Rice recalls him bowling one of the most hostile spells he's seen against the one-time England player, Paul Parker.

'For about 10 deliveries, Parker didn't know which part of his body to rub first. Richard was hitting him everywhere and you sensed the batsman was longing to get out and back to the pavilion for safety. Funnily enough, Parker did get out, but not in the way you might expect. He played a superb hook at one of Richard's short ones, getting on top of the ball and hitting it down. To his amazement, Tim Robinson took a blinding low catch backward of square!'

Hadlee was able to tell his rapt radio audience in New Zealand that at half-term he was bang on schedule . . .

449 runs and 57 wickets. Each week he would broadcast over the telephone to his local radio station 3ZB. The interest on the other side of the world was possibly even greater than in England!

He also had to report that he had turned down the invitation to tour Pakistan with New Zealand during the English winter. It brought to an end his unbroken run of Test appearances stretching back eight years.

It was disappointing for everyone concerned, but there was no way I could face a tour like that so soon after the English season. Like Botham pulling out of the England tour of India, I felt I must have time away from the game. It's like a machine that needs servicing and greasing every now and again. Ignore that and it will let you down.

The last time I went to Pakistan in 1976, I lost a lot of weight, as many players do. I couldn't possibly afford to put myself in a position where my health was at risk, especially after what happened at home last November. I'm determined that I will never again allow myself to become mentally or physically exhausted.

Scores of 41 against Somerset at Trent Bridge, 70 at Worcester and 56 at home against Derbyshire failed to make up for the run famine which came in between. Hadlee had planned to score three centuries. So far he'd managed one. After the Derbyshire game, only seven matches remained.

A series of quite superb bowling feats had brought him to within twenty of the target already and his average was a remarkable 13.95. One of his best performances was in the controversial two-day win over Worcestershire at Trent Bridge. It was an unusual match in several respects. For a start, Worcester had the temerity to bat first . . . the only side to take that gamble at Trent Bridge all season.

The decision backfired sensationally. By lunchtime, on Saturday, 14 July, they had collapsed to 56—6. For once it wasn't Hadlee doing the damage, but young Andy Pick, the local youngster standing in for Saxelby. He ripped out the off stump of the much-fancied Dipak Patel who was being tipped for England honours, and had Kapil Dev taken behind off a real flier for 0. Worcestershire rallied to 138 and by the time the match ended at 7.45 that sunny evening, Notts had lost two wickets as well.

The fall of twelve wickets on the first day prompted the umpires, Ray Julian and John Jameson to report the pitch for 'uneven bounce'. Before play resumed on Monday, Bernard Flack, the Inspector of Pitches came to have a look. Notts manager, Ken Taylor said at the time: 'Maybe the wicket wasn't up to scratch but I honestly believe we were unlucky. Preparing pitches isn't an exact science and there are times when we make mistakes.'

Hadlee made no mistake in the Worcestershire second innings, taking 5−61 from eighteen overs. Six more at home against Lancashire, one at Worcester and seven in the shock defeat by Derbyshire at Trent Bridge brought up the eighty victims. The statistics were overshadowed by the result of the game.

With half centuries from Robinson, Randall, Rice and Hadlee and 42 from French, Notts were apparently sitting pretty with a first innings total of 361. For Trent Bridge it was excellent. Even better when Derbyshire folded at 139 with Hadlee taking 4−30 from thirteen overs. Rice enforced the follow-on with every reason to believe that his side could swiftly make up ground on the championship leaders, Essex. (Leicestershire, as predicted by Rice, had faltered badly.)

The pitch was easing. Kim Barnett, another tipped for England recognition made 90 in the Derbyshire second innings, but worse from the Notts point of view, Geoff Miller and Roger Finney, the number seven and eight batsmen, added 135 for the seventh wicket. The Notts out-cricket had gone to pieces. Considering that Derbyshire totalled 381, Hadlee's analysis of twenty-five overs, nine maidens, 3−47 was outstanding.

To win and close the gap on the leaders, Notts had a comfortable-looking target of 160 in thirty-five overs. Chasing targets at Trent Bridge hadn't been one of their fortes that season . . . the John Player League performances at home undoubtedly cost them the chance of that title as well. Rash hitting against the spin attack

of Miller and Dallas Moir left Notts 29 runs adrift.
Spectators couldn't believe it. To rub salt in the wound,
Essex had beaten Middlesex brilliantly to extend their
advantage at the top of the chart. Hadlee was as insensed
as anyone:

We were pathetic. Our fielding hovered between the brilliant and the burlesque. We gave so many runs away that day that it wasn't true. Some guys didn't even seem to be trying. The sloppiness carried over into our second innings performance. I was as guilty as anyone, getting out for ten just when we needed someone to steady the ship.

By the time we got to the Middlesex game, the 1,000 runs were looking out of range. With seven games left I still needed 330. I was going to have to strike out and hope for the best. Don't forget, I had only budgeted for playing twenty out of the twenty-four games, and seventeen had gone! Clearly I wasn't going to do it in twenty games. I was well and truly up the creek. The weather was the saviour. I would have four more matches than I had budgeted for and that would make all the difference.

Of course I could have played against Oxford and Cambridge and collected a lot of cheap runs which would have counted. I never play those games and I wasn't going to start now. I also missed the matches against Sri Lanka and the West Indies. Only championship matches were allowed to count.

Shortly before the Middlesex game at Lords, Rice told
Hadlee that the only hope was to hit a double century, so
he did!

8

Double Century Breakthrough

NOTTINGHAMSHIRE v MIDDLESEX at Lords
August 11 & 13

Notts first innings:

R. T. Robinson	hit wkt b Daniel	0
M. Newell	lbw b Cowans	3
D. W. Randall	b Daniel	11
C. E. B. Rice	c Metson b Daniel	2
P. Johnson	c Metson b Williams	36
R. J. Hadlee	not out	210
B. N. French	b Cowans	26
E. E. Hemmings	c Metson b Williams	1
K. Saxelby	c Slack b Daniel	4
K. E. Cooper	b Williams	3
P. M. Such	lbw Cowans	16
	Extras	32
	Total (86.4 overs)	344

Fall of wickets: 1-3 2-15 3-17 4-17 5-141 6-248 7-261 8-268 9-287 10-344.

Middlesex bowling figures

Daniel	22	3	85	4
Cowans	23.4	1	82	3
Williams	16	2	64	3
Edmonds	20	4	61	0
Emburey	5	1	20	0

Details of Hadlee's Innings:

50 in 48 minutes:	35 balls:	8 fours:	1 six
100 in 130 minutes:	93 balls:	16 fours:	1 six
150 in 207 minutes:	151 balls:	22 fours:	1 six
200 in 337 minutes:	242 balls:	24 fours:	1 six
210 in 356 minutes:	261 balls:	24 fours:	1 six

The breakthrough could not have come at a more unexpected moment. On 11 August, at Lords, Middlesex won the toss and decided to bat, clearly fancying their chances of creeping up on the two leading counties, Essex and Notts.

It was tough going. Hadlee and Saxelby were in tandem and Cooper came on first change to bowl five consecutive maidens. Clive Radley resisted for nearly three hours, scoring 50, but Middlesex crumbled to a first innings total of 152. Saxelby's figures were 5—43 and Hadlee, for the umpteenth time that season, collected another bag of four in his twenty overs. He now needed thirteen wickets for the 100.

On a seaming wicket, Wayne Daniel was too much for the Notts early batsmen to cope with. The big West Indian had Robinson out, hit wicket for 0; Randall bowled for 11, and Rice caught behind for 2. In between, Norman Cowans, operating from the other end trapped young Mike Newell leg before with only 3 to his name and Notts were teetering at 17—4. Hardly the time for heroics, more a case of someone getting their nose over the ball and repairing the damage. That's not Hadlee's style.

I was quietly fuming because all our hard work seemed to be going down the drain. There were twenty minutes to tea and as I walked to the wicket, I said to the umpire, David Shepherd that if I was still there at the break, I'd have twenty runs. Eighteen of them came from Daniel's first over! It felt good. They were bowling to a very attacking field so there was plenty of space to hit and even miscue. Just the right conditions for me, you might say. I only had to connect and it was four with all those men up.

At tea, I was on 26 and Shepherd gave me a wink as we walked in. Paul Johnston was at the other end and playing very sensibly. In the last session of the day, the runs just kept coming. It was one of those days when I couldn't do a thing wrong. Middlesex didn't bowl very well, either too full a length or too short with plenty of fielders still around the bat. My sole thought was to get as many runs as I could while it lasted. Against an international attack of Cowans, Daniel, Phil Edmunds and Emburey, you could disappear at any moment. The first 50 came in very quick time — forty-eight minutes with eight fours and a six off thirty-five deliveries. The figures are etched in my mind. Everything after 50 became a bonus. I wouldn't say I was thinking of the double century at that stage, but when it's your day, you begin to feel that the sky's the limit.

I gave one chance to Cowans at long-off from Edmunds bowling just after reaching my half century, but that was all. When Middlesex pushed mid-on, mid-off and cover back to stop me crashing the ball through, I simply took the ones and twos. In the latter part of my innings, the boundaries were few and far between.

I was running out of partners. Johnson went for 36 then Bruce French stayed for a while and at stumps on the first day, we'd recovered to 195 − 5 with me 127 not out. I was only 15 runs short of my personal best in England. The key to the whole thing was Peter Such, who was last man in. On the second day, I'd scored 184 when he came to the wicket. Now Peter had a career best of five and a batting average of one! I didn't panic. He's a sensible lad and I told him just to play straight while I tried to farm the bowling. We needed thirteen runs to reach 300 and pick up another valuable batting point. It was mid-afternoon and the chances of me reaching that double century looked a little slim.

To his eternal credit, 'Suchie' fooled everyone, including himself. Not only did we get that final batting point, but we actually put on 57 for the last wicket! I'd never seen him hit a boundary, but when Cowans bowled one down the legside, Such nipped it round behind square for four. Then he poked one between the wicket-keeper and slip for another. We just kept talking to each other at the end of the overs. My confidence was spreading to him and I had no worries about him towards the end. I was taking a run off the first ball of

88

the over sometimes. Fortunately, Such got some protection from the umpires who warned the bowlers about short-pitched deliveries. Poor old Peter was getting hit all over the body. I can't speak highly enough of his contribution.

From my personal point of view, it was magnificent. Thanks to him I was able to press on past the 200 mark. The pacemen were giving me the works with the short stuff. It didn't worry me because I had room to smack the ball over the slips or paddle it round square. Once I reached the double century, Suchie was more relieved than I was. It was the turning point of the whole season for me. Scoring 200 was worth four matches. It took me to 880 and I knew then that I would achieve my ambition. The dream, the obsession had become a reality. All that was left was the final push for home. I wasn't tired after that knock, just 'pleasantly weary'!

Just to gild the lily, Cooper turned in his career-best bowling performance of 8-44 when Middlesex batted again, and Notts had beaten Mike Gatting's star-studded team by an innings and 43 runs with a day to spare. It placed them twenty points behind the leaders, Essex, still with that game in hand.

News of Hadlee's breathtaking innings spread quickly across the globe. He received this letter from his friend and mentor, Grahame Felton, the motivation expert:

119 Mount Pleasant Road,
Christchurch, N.Z.
August 15, 1984.

Dear Richard, Karen and Nicholas,

Great to hear from you over there. The press reports are avidly searched for and read by the Feltons and today's is truly a gem. Well done indeed. Richard, this really sounds like the winner making his play. No doubt you simulated the double century and saw yourself acknowledging the credits from the pavilion and your team mates . . . Very weary but pleasantly weary!

Remember, winners don't get tired, we let our robots do that and draw on our chemical reserves of opiate, enzymes, adrenalin and hormones which are stored in our body pharmacy, and awaiting trigger release by our optimism. You know you have the ability—tons of it—the thing that makes you the total winner is believing in yourself (esteem), that deep-down inner feeling of your own worth, and feeling that you deserve it. Now the 1000/100 double is yours man! You desire it, deserve it, see yourself having it (expectancy and simulation) and have set your goal just out of reach, but not out of sight. You will now make that final effort which will give it to you.

Six matches for 120 runs and twelve wickets which you should aim to achieve in the first three games! What we expect we generally get, so start the simulation going now with those runs and wickets as your expectancy.

There will NOT be any injury—instead you'll be constantly thinking: Fit, healthy, energetic, alive and enjoying every moment, even the crises which, as the Chinese say, are welcome and dangerous opportunities. They make the achieving that much sweeter.

Go get it, Richard and make it the double win—you win and we win—Karen, Nicholas, the family, the Feltons and N.Z.!

Weather generally cold and wintry but snow on the mountains—good for ski industry. Days are lengthening so roll on summer. Our best wishes to you all there, God bless,
   Grahame and Doreen.
Winners make it happen—losers let it!

Felton even corrected a newspaper cutting in which Hadlee was quoted as saying he had 'a bit of luck' making his 210 not out. Felton wrote underneath: 'No luck, Rich!' Hadlee went on air in New Zealand, publicly thanking him for his help and guidance throughout the season.

His influence on my cricket and my life have been immense. So soon after my breakdown I was able to put tremendous pressure on myself and come through smiling. I had this superb desire to win and prove myself the best and a lot of that was directly down to Grahame. Without his inspiration, I doubt I'd have made it.

9

England, Poor England!

It was during Hadlee's glorious summer that England were being roasted by Clive Lloyd's West Indians. As much as any other casual spectator, Hadlee was surprised by the 5-0 margin of victory. It seemed to him that too many people accepted the West Indies team as invincible, and perhaps surrendered a little too meekly. His own experiences against the best side in the world are limited — the forthcoming New Zealand tour of the Caribbean is his first — but he believes that the West Indian team which lost in New Zealand in 1979-80 was possibly even stronger than the current one, albeit without Viv Richards. There was Kallicharran and Rowe in the middle order, Collis King as the all-rounder, and that most fearsome quartet of bowlers, Garner, Holding, Roberts and Croft.

New Zealand are the last side to have beaten the West Indies, winning the First Test at Dunedin by a solitary wicket, and drawing the remaining two encounters. It was an ill-tempered series marred by unsavoury incidents like Michael Holding's destruction of the stumps after a caught behind appeal had been turned down. It was also clouded in allegations of biased umpires. Be that as it may, New Zealand did what no other country has managed since. Prominent in that success was Richard Hadlee. In the victorious Test, he claimed eleven wickets in the match and scored 51 in the first innings. The slogger had matured into a quality batsman. His average for the series was 44.5 and included a century in the Second Test at Christchurch.

Inevitably, he topped the New Zealand bowling averages, taking 19 wickets at a cost of 19 runs each.

There's no doubt England should have done much better than they did. The one thing that stands out in my mind is the quality of their bowling. It simply wasn't controlled enough for that level of competition. They didn't seem to have a plan of attack. Against batsmen of that calibre, it's fatal, as we saw. We must however put the thing into proportion. The rebels who toured South Africa were missing and that has severely weakened England's team in the last three years.

In a way it's a good thing because it enables the team to start rebuilding, rather like the Aussies when they lost Lillee, Marsh and Chappell. England have been able to give a number of youngsters a chance. They're probably not good enough initially but the experience should help them in the future. If England had been able to pick the rebels it might have been a very different story. Next summer they'll become available again, all being well, and Graham Gooch and John Emburey will come into consideration. Possibly John Lever as well, and there's Peter Willey, a gutsy and professional cricketer for whom I've a lot of admiration. He would balance the side nicely, batting at five or six and bowling his off-spinners. With four or five of the banned players back in the reckoning, England should be able to restore their credibility.

I felt for David Gower. Giving him the captaincy was a good decision because England have to look to the future. It'll be 2-3 years I reckon before England becomes a dominant force again, and Gower needs that period to learn the art of captaincy and to mould a youthful team into something that can compete. Playing your first series against the West Indies is about the toughest baptism you could have — a nightmare for any captain.

Gower is without doubt a world-class batsman. He has a ton of time in which to play the ball and if you bowl straight at him or stray a little down the leg side, you'll get hit. The same if you drop it too short. But for a batsman of his class, he has a big weakness on or outside the off stump. To be fair, many players are weak in that area, but Gower gives the impression of being very casual and loose, especially early in the innings. After an initial run of success, teams have worked him out and know exactly where to bowl to him. You fill the offside with three slips and two gullies and if you're good enough and consistent enough to bowl around off stump, he'll play and miss and eventually get out. The number of times he's caught in the area is incredible. Now that weakness has been exposed, his career has started to change quite dramatically.

We sorted him out in New Zealand because we had our plan of attack. Even in the series in England last summer, although he got a hundred and a seventy, we could have had him out cheaply most times if we'd held onto the catches. In New Zealand he had a miserable time. He didn't seem to know where his off-stump was. In the Christchurch Test I remember he shouldered arms to one that I bowled and was out lbw. Then he got caught in the slips-gully area a couple of times, and bowled off-stump on another occasion.

Funnily enough, I don't usually like bowling to left-handers. I like to get close to the wicket and swing the ball or move it away from the right-hander towards the slips. If you do that to a left-hander of course it goes leg side. That's why so many of them are good off their pads. A lot of bowlers naturally drift that way. To deliver to someone like Gower, you've got to change your action and your mechanics. That means coming wider of the crease and pushing it across the body. That way you lose quite a lot of pace, bodywork and movement.

Graham Gooch will have to be considered one of the best batsmen in England. His record speaks for itself, and last summer his contribution to Essex's championship title was enormous. He was the country's top run-getter, came third in the averages with 67-odd and won many games for his county, especially when chasing targets. He would come in and hit a very quick and efficient hundred. England certainly need someone like Gooch to open the innings. Personally, I like bowling to him. His technique is a little different in the sense that he stands tall and upright with his bat in the air before you deliver the ball. He has a natural tendency to plant his foot down in the middle of the pitch and anything straight will be blasted through the 'V' between mid-on and mid-off. We've worked him out now. We know that you can't bowl straight at him. You have to make him chase the ball. If it's aimed outside the off stump, his foot is still down the middle of the pitch and when he brings down his bat, he's often fishing at it.

His head is out of line, and the number of times that he can be 'nicked out' (that is, caught behind), are considerable. For Notts, Kevin Cooper is usually the bowler who gets Gooch to nick the catch, but he's played and missed an extraordinary number of times against me. We have exposed his weakness although he's a prolific run scorer. I just wonder how many other clubs have worked it out the way we have. It doesn't mean that he won't go and score a hundred against us, but at least we have a plan of attack. I have a memory box in my head like many international bowlers and I know what needs to be done against most batsmen.

Some of the hardest guys to bowl against are number eleven batsmen. If you try to york them or just bowl them out, they somehow manage to hit the balls that are on the wicket. Anything off-line they play and miss because they're not good enough to get a touch.

There's no batsman in the world that would worry me unduly, and I don't mean that in a big-headed way. It's just that I would back myself to get anyone out. It doesn't mean I always will, but I believe that I CAN and on my day I will. There are some players who give you more of a challenge than others. Geoff Boycott for one. If you get him out (and I haven't too often) you know you've really earned his wicket. He's getting on a bit now but every year, he's up there in the averages. I've found him probably the hardest guy I've ever bowled to. He's a player that every bowler must respect because he's so professional. His application, concentration and dedication are second to none and he never gives anything away. All he wants to do is occupy the crease and score runs and he's prepared to wear the bowler down to get what he wants. He knows that I will bowl six or seven overs in a spell so he gets his head down and sees me out for that spell. With another bowler, it might be ten overs and Boycott will know. This can go on for hour after hour and probably day after day.

Boycott's so run-hungry that he won't take any chances. If you do beat his bat and get through his defences, it's a major triumph. On the other hand, he's not the sort of player who will tear you apart, so you have the illusion of being in control. He's happy to play maiden overs, nudging and deflecting singles until a bad ball comes along, then he hits it for four. His style militates against him a little there because he would probably receive fewer bad balls than most. Bowlers know that the only way to play him is to peg away and wait for something to happen. You're very fortunate if it does. His judgement is so good that anything fractionally outside off-stump he will leave alone.

Most of the things that are said about Ian Botham and myself are true. There IS a deadly rivalry between us on the field of play because Both is statistically the greatest all-rounder in the game. Having passed the 300 Test wicket and 4,000 Test runs milestone, he's earned that title. No-one will beat him. He'll probably go down in history as a better all-rounder than Gary Sobers — at least that's what the record books will say. He is a totally different cricketer from me. We can both be matchwinners but he is essentially a crowd-pleaser. He is not consistent with it. He can win a match with the ball or bat as he did against the Aussies at Headingley, Edgbaston and Old Trafford, but it's not as though you can rely on him. To me professionalism is consistency — a bowler bowling line and length, a batsman getting regular fifties and sixties plus a liberal sprinkling of big scores and an average at the end of the day of about fifty. I'm not suggesting that Both's not a pro, but to me, that's what a pro should be looking to do.

The rivalry between us is natural. He's the number one all-rounder and doesn't want to be knocked off his perch. The fact that we played two successive series against each other in England and New Zealand and I beat him for 'Man of the Series' is a feather in my cap. It's something I badly wanted to do and something he wouldn't like at all. It was a dent in his pride. I've had very little to do with him off the field until the all-rounders competition at Taunton which followed our nailbiting championship match against Somerset. We communicated more then than in the previous six years. Let's say we struck up a very tentative relationship and I found him OK.

As an opponent, he gives you a chance when he's batting against you. Like me, he loves to whack the ball away and go for his shots. At the same time, he can tear you apart. You can be bowling well then all of a sudden your figures are a mess. The honours between us I guess are about even. I've got him out a couple of times, but he tore me apart in the one-day international at Old Trafford in 1978. I came away with 1−70 from eleven overs and he was responsible for the last 35 off two overs! Yes he's smacked me all around the ground, but I've done the same to him.

Early on in his career, Botham was a very fine bowler, a genuine swing bowler who could move the ball both ways and use the bouncer with devastating effect. What you have to remember though is that he got many of his wickets during the World Series era when a lot of top players were out of Test cricket. Having said that, he still had to get people out, beat his opponents and score runs against some very good bowlers. His record in the last few years however hasn't been so impressive and that's coincided with those top class players returning to Test cricket.

On top of that, Botham has got heavier and there may be a serious question mark over his fitness. He'll still bowl plenty of overs but he's much bigger than he was and I'm sure that's blunted his effectiveness. He doesn't swing the ball half as much as he used to. If anything, he's tending to angle the ball in towards the batsman instead of moving it in the air. Also, he's probably overdoing the variation and I think it's a mistake to use the short-pitched ball so much at his reduced pace. The wickets still come, but they're costing him a lot more. There's a little more predictability about him because he's lost movement and speed. Nevertheless, Both is a player you'd still be delighted to have on your side because he can turn a match even now. We saw against the West Indies last summer that he can still pull a few surprises.

My old clubmate Derek Randall is an amazing character. Talk about a man on a hot wire! If people only knew what he was like in the dressing room they wouldn't believe it. Derek's a wreck. He 'psyches' himself out before he starts, worrying about how to play this or that bowler. He has nothing worked out. The opposite of me I suppose. Come to think, it would be interesting to see him on one of those motivation courses. I don't think he'd last the distance! I have a lot of sympathy for Derek because his nervous disposition is against him all the time. To have played forty-seven times for his country with an average of 30-plus is a terrific achievement.

I don't think England could possibly have taken him to India though I know many of his fans were annoyed about his exclusion from the party. His form really hasn't been good enough or consistent enough to merit selection. The trouble is that you can't rely on Derek. At Trent Bridge, I don't think we DO rely on him very much. Sometimes he can look world class, other times, less than ordinary. He played beautifully against us in New Zealand, scoring two centuries, but he hasn't very often turned a match for Notts. He is certainly not a pressure player. He scores runs either in the first innings of a match, perhaps when we're looking for bonus points and he's got 100 overs to do it. But if he's batting against the clock and chasing a target, or even if a certain bowler comes on, he goes to pieces. He lacks confidence entirely.

Derek has been very badly handled by England. Each time they fail, he seems to have been the sacrificial offering, the only one left out the next time, or excluded from an overseas tour. Putting him in to bat at number three or even as opener is senseless and unfair. Technically, he's deficient against express bowling. Against medium pace or spin, he's a class player but higher up the order is a waste. The position for him would have been at five or six as it was in New Zealand. He needs to come in when the bowlers are a bit tired, the ball is older and the pitch flatter. It's so obvious, I'm surprised the England selectors haven't realised it.

His main problem is that he doesn't believe in his own ability. Being dropped so many times by England has only made it worse. Derek has told me playing for his country is his one big passion. He doesn't mind where he bats, as long as he plays. Being left out really hurts.

97

Spectators will enjoy watching him in the field clowning, and diving about, anything to burn up nervous energy. They think it's great fun, but in the dressing room he's a quivering bag of nerves who doesn't give himself a chance to perform. He'll never sit in one position for very long — always jumping about and fidgeting. He's been involved in so many run-outs that it's become a dressing room joke that he practises them in the mirror before he goes out to bat. The conversation goes something like this: 'Come on Rags, there's a single there . . . yes . . . no . . . wait . . . oops . . . sorry!' Though it isn't his position, he'd be better in some ways getting out there and opening the innings, at least some of the pressure would be released. Batting lower down the order must be murder for him. He's hopping about waiting, watching, panicking if he sees the ball beat the bat. You'd think he'd never played the game before.

I've noticed when batting with him in limited over matches that he's blissfully unaware of the state of play. He seems to have no idea how many runs we need per over, or how many we might have chalked up in the previous over. Amazing really, unless he's just taking the mickey. You're never quite sure about that. I remember we were getting towards the end of a pre-season friendly against Derbyshire and needed 6 to win with three overs to go. Derek got it into his head that he'd got to hit the bowler for 6 to finish it. In this case it was Paul Newman, the Derby paceman. For no reason at all, Derek took a mighty swipe and walloped the bloke out of sight for an enormous 6 to finish the game. Totally unnecessary but totally Randall.

In the field he's a constant problem for his captain. You never know where he is. Clive will put him in the covers and a few minutes later he's fielding somewhere completely different. In the last match at Taunton, he got so fed up he took Derek aside and told him he would make it easy for him (Derek). 'You see that signboard for salted peanuts around the boundary?' said Rice. 'Just stand in front of the nuts and we'll know where you are!' That was alright for about thirty seconds until he moved again! What can you do with him? He's predictable at being unpredictable, as his wife Liz says. One moment he can be quietly washing the dishes and the next he'll throw a cup in the air and catch it behind his back one-handed. Or he'll be sitting in the lounge reading a newspaper then suddenly decide to go for a swim twenty-five miles away. He'd think nothing of driving twenty-five miles just for that.

The only genuine pressure-player in the England side is Allan Lamb, and in my view he shouldn't be in the side at all! He's about as English as me. In fact I'm more English because at least I'm a colonial. Surely Englishmen are born, not made, otherwise there's absolutely no point in having one nation pitted against another. I think it's grossly unfair that a player born outside the country with an accent as foreign as you could every wish to hear, should be able to qualify for the national team just because of some tenuous parental connection and a period of years spent in his new homeland. It's completely false and makes a mockery of the system. I've no personal axe to grind against Lamb but it's about as daft as my mate Clive Rice playing for England. He's going through the qualification process, so one day, technically, he should be available. It seems crazy to talk about reducing the number of overseas cricketers in one breath, then allowing Lamb and Chris Smith to play for England in the next. What gets me is the way the coloured nations change their standards once Lamb becomes a so-called Englishman. All of a sudden it's OK to play with and against him whereas before they couldn't. The system is riddled with hypocrisy and double standards.

We get the same type of thing happening in New Zealand soccer. English players who can't make the grade come over to play for league sides. After a period of years, they too qualify for the national side in World Cup matches, etc. It's unfair on the locally-born players, the same way that it's unfair on English batsmen to have to move over for Lamb and Smith. You'd have to apply that also to Kepler Wessels of Australia—a fine Aussie accent he's got!

Having said all that, Lamb is an excellent batsman. He proved against the West Indies last summer that he's made of strong stuff. He was the only England player to come through the series with any credit. Invariably he was thrown into the firing line when England had lost quick wickets to

Marshall and co. and to come out of that series with three centuries against his name was guts and batsmanship of the highest order. Lamb's not an easy opponent. You have to work him out, look for his weakness. If he has one it's that he can be a little carefree, rather like Gower. He's a touch vulnerable early on like a lot of players, but if you don't nail him then, he's going to get a big score as likely as not.

Gazing around the counties, I don't think there's any talent the England selectors have missed. They've given just about everyone a chance who deserved it. I would make a plea though for Dennis Amiss. I know he was one of the South African rebels, but the selectors could do worse than consider him against the Australians this coming summer. Even at forty-one, he's still a class player and finished the season with well over 2,000 runs and an average of almost 56. If you look at the history of English cricket, one or two batsmen like Cowdrey and Close have been worth their place at forty plus. Amiss is a superb player of spin bowling and medium pace and I believe he's sorted out most of the quicks after his early traumas.

I must just say a word too about my Notts colleagues, Chris Broad and Tim Robinson. I was very disappointed for Chris that he missed the India tour. He did nothing wrong against the West Indies or Sri Lanka. He and Fowler were thrown in at the deep end to open the innings for England, and Chris went and scored a half century on his debut. That takes some spirit. The pair never really failed all series, though they weren't a screaming success either. Nobody was. I think that having sweated it out against the most hostile attack in the world, Chris should have been rewarded with a place on the tour. He was shattered by the decision to leave him out and well he might be.

I can see the thinking behind the omission. Chris isn't at his strongest against spin and the selectors obviously felt that spin would be the biggest problem in India. One or two other players should have been omitted as well on that basis. Martyn Moxon handles spin worse than Chris Broad and he hasn't in my opinion produced the form to merit a tour. I'm very surprised at that selection.

As for Tim Robinson, well he's had a couple of good

seasons – 1400 runs in 1983 and more than 2000 last season. What's more he got a lot of those runs at Trent Bridge which is a real test of a batsman. That meant that he must be worth selection. I thought he might have to wait a year or two but he's got his chance and I wish him the very best of luck.

On the bowling side, England haven't really got any class speed merchants, apart from Norman Cowans. He's the only genuine quickie in the country. You'd put Graham Dilley into that category if he was fit, but he's got technical problems as well. Cowans has had a raw deal. He's another one who's been mis-handled. As a youngster he went to Australia and did quite well, taking six wickets in an innings in one Test. He came back with a reputation, but he's been confused and spoiled by too many people trying to tell him how to bowl. They go on about the way he collapses his front leg when he delivers and all that. No wonder he goes backwards instead of progressing. Then he's brought back against the West Indies on a slow flat track at Old Trafford which knocks his confidence even further. By the time he's dropped again for the next Test, the poor chap's on his knees. In order to rebuild his confidence, they had to pick him for India or risk setting him back years. Yet he was a bright hope. I was impressed with him in New Zealand, but I think Willis then Gower have handled him badly.

I'd pick Cowans out because he's got a big heart. He charges in off a longish run and lets the ball go at real speed. He's got enormous potential if he's guided in the right direction.

Instead of concentrating on the negative aspects of his play, people should encourage his good points. There's no doubt he's the pick of the bunch if you want a real express.

Mind you, there's a lot of nonsense talked about pace. Of course it helps if you're really quick. The batsmen will respect you a lot more. But it's no use if you're not accurate with it. Sometimes it's just as useful to be able to do something with the ball. That's why I like the look of Paul Allott and Neil Foster. Allott has improved a lot and does the basics. He gets in close to the wicket like Foster, bowls wicket to wicket which means there's a good chance of lbw's and clean

101

bowled's and, if he can nip it away a bit, the catch to the wicket-keeper. They're both trying to bowl maidens which is important. Neither is prepared to give away five or six runs an over whereas Botham is. He probably over-attacks. He'll bowl a four-ball every over. He's still likely to get you out, but at the end of twenty overs he's gone for 80 runs. In contrast, Allott will have given away half that amount, and still picked up four wickets.

Foster has a good action. When he gets bigger and broader he'll be that much more effective. Basically, he's got everything it takes. It's just a matter of time whether he makes it or not. You don't produce world class players overnight. You have to give it three or four years. When I started my career in 1971-72 it took me five years to come of age. I remember Glenn Turner saying on the 1976 tour of Pakistan and India that I'd grown up. Since then, my success has been remarkable, in terms of strike rate, wickets, confidence, the lot. Cowans has only been on the scene for three years and Foster two. Their potential should start to be realised any time now, though it could be another year before they get into their true rhythm and find the consistency that demands automatic selection.

Of the other pacemen England have tried, I don't honestly believe that Jonathan Agnew has a lot to offer at present, though he's a very effective county bowler. With Leicestershire having bowlers like Andy Roberts, Gordon Parsons, Paddy Clift and George Ferris, it's meant keeping Agnew back. He has a good action but he hasn't filled out enough and doesn't seem consistent enough for the highest grade. I sincerely hope I'm wrong.

Richard Ellison I quite like. He's been brought into the tour to replace Botham and that's deserved because he's the only genuine swing bowler I've come across in England. He probably swings the ball a little too early which makes him predictable, but not many bowlers get the ball to leave the bat these days. The reason is that one-day cricket has killed outswing. Bowlers, especially in the latter part of the innings, have got to come wide of the wicket and arrow the ball towards the leg side. They open up their bodies and become 'arm' bowlers. When they go back into the three-day game, they find it hard to adjust. Ellison is probably unique and a useful batsman too. Whether or not he develops we'll have to wait and see.

10

Sacred Island

Sri Lanka's success against England last summer didn't surprise Hadlee:

Much to our regret, Gary Sobers' team beat us in the World Cup in England, and, as a member of the first side to play a Test series out there,I can tell you that they are quite a force. Although we won the three-match series 2-0, I was impressed with the facilities on the Sacred Island, though not so much with the living conditions outside Colombo.

It was the first time in New Zealand history that we'd won a series away from home, since 1969. While Sri Lanka are new to Test cricket and have a lower rating than any other Test side, it was still gratifying to do well on foreign soil.

Let me warn future tourists that conditions are very taxing. Apart from the intense heat and high humidity, we had to put up with unresponsive pitches, largely unknown opponents, a crowded itinerary, inconsistent umpiring, dietary problems, excitable crowds and variable hotel standards! Perhaps the biggest problem was boredom. There was nothing to do outside of cricket and the tour became rather like a prison sentence — we had to do our 'time'. That sounds pretty negative, but there were compensations.

The Sacred Island is fantastically beautiful, as European tourists have discovered. Our stay at Galle on the southwest coast reminded me of Fiji and Raratonga in the Cook Islands — golden sandy beaches; palm trees; still, turquoise seas. The hill country is quite superb. It took us seven hours by bus to reach Nuwra Eliya from Colombo. We travelled only 130 miles up narrow winding roads. The countryside was lush and green with tropical rain forest, millions of acres of tea plantations and hundreds of waterfalls.

All the way, the roadside was littered with stalls — people selling everything from soft drinks, fruit and vegetables, flowers, ornaments and home-made clothing. There were many examples of British Imperialism left in Sri Lanka. The tudor-style hotel at Nuwra Eliya was suitably named the Grand. Obviously, there was plenty of poverty and deprivation too.

Most of the hotels were excellent, especially in Colombo. The Oberoi Lanka would rate alongside any that I've stayed in around the world. At Galle, the accommodation was more than adequate, but, just as in the hotel at Kandy, we had to sleep in mosquito nets — fine until one of the little perishers gets inside!

We were happy with the meals both at the cricket grounds and in the hotels. We could get steaks, chicken and fresh vegetables almost everywhere we went. I found it essential to have a couple of bowls of soup each day to keep up my strength. The food problems we had were at Radella where the waiters failed to understand that we could grow tired of pineapples and bananas every lunchtime!

After the first two weeks of the five-week tour, we began to question the itinerary. It was clear that we were doing too much travelling, and that we were being restricted to some of the cooler areas of the country like Galle with its sea breeze, Radella, up in the mountains, and Kandy, where the First Test was staged. That was all very well, but the last two Tests were scheduled for Colombo where the heat was overpowering. We had no chance to acclimatise. It seemed that if Sri Lanka could hold on for a draw at Kandy, they fancied their chances at Colombo, knowing that we'd be unused to the conditions.

Our opening practice matches were a farce. At Galle the outfield was bumpy and dangerous and water seeped under the covers, reducing it to a two-day match. At Radella, the locals warned us that the rains would come again, and sure enough, at the appointed hour of two o'clock, the heavens opened. That was the end of that!

After my illness, I'd been very wary about health risks on the equator, but I'd needn't have worried. With the exception of Martin Crowe who developed tummy trouble, we all kept in good shape. Full marks to 'Doc' Richard Edmund who made sure we ate the right foods and drank bottled water. Anything uncooked or without a skin was strictly taboo. As well, the 'Doc' shovelled malaria tablets down us with the warning that we could still die if the right mossie got its teeth into us. From then on, Richard became known as 'Doctor Doom'.

The crowds in Sri Lanka were something else . . . usually very small but very biased. For the one-day games, we'd attract 10-15,000, but for the Tests, the gate was much smaller. They became very excited when their bowlers took a wicket, and the firecrackers would go off if a Sri Lankan batsman scored runs. The contrast when we batted was incredible. You could have heard a pin drop! I came in for the treatment when I was bowling. They didn't like my bouncers. Up would go the chorus: 'Go home Hadlee.' Little did they know that I'd have been only too happy to oblige!

Once, they turned against their own man. In the first test, Duleep Mendis, the Sri Lankan captain failed in both innings against my bowling. Some of the spectators were delighted. They booed Mendis because they wanted Warnapura to skipper the side. Unfortunately, Warnapura had been banned for a quarter of a century for playing in South Africa! At the end of that game, riot police with tear gas were brought in to disperse the crowd. Bricks and stones were thrown and both teams needed police escorts. Some of the Sri Lankan players were very concerned for their own safety after losing the Test. I gathered there was a strong undercurrent of ethnic and religious hostility between different parts of the island, as has been proved since. Mob violence didn't seem to be far under the surface.

Against that, the general conditions and the grounds were well up to standard. We had spacious dressing rooms and good ventilation. The room attendant, a chap called Siree, did a marvellous job looking after us throughout the tour.

Although he weighed only six stone or so, he managed all the baggage himself and insisted on carrying two cricket 'coffins' at a time.

The Test venues were impressive. I was surprised how many grounds in Colombo were suitable for staging Tests. The ground maintenance and the scoreboard facilities were top-class. All three Test pitches were exceptional. They were on the slow side but the bounce was consistent. At the beginning of the tour it seemed that the spinners would enjoy themselves. At Kandy, the ball did turn but at the Sinhalese and Colombo Cricket Club grounds, there was precious little help.

Over the series, the seamers were the most successful and the swing bowlers had a great time in the heavy atmosphere. John and Ravi dominated the home attack with their fast-medium deliveries, while I managed to dominate the whole series, taking twenty-three wickets at a cost of 10 runs each. Bowling in short spells, I got the ball to swing and bounce. The Sri Lankans were unable to cope with the variation. My success surprised me because I had to work very hard to keep going in the heat. Luckily, I had some excellent catches taken in the slips. On top of that, the Sri Lankans soon came to fear me and I made maximum use of the psychological advantage. (An added bonus was the 'Kookuburra' ball they played with out there. I was used to that make at home.)

The Sri Lankan attitude to the series was defensive. They may have felt they could win the Second Test, but as the series progressed, they played for safety and slowed the games to a crawl. We played five and a half hours each day with a drinks interlude every forty-five minutes. Mendis altered his field at least twice an over and insisted on having his bowlers on the boundary when they'd finished their over. Consequently, it took ages for them to get back to their marks to start a new one. They were averaging only twelve overs an hour even with the spinners in the attack. Only 70-75 were being bowled in the day, so the batting side was lucky to score 180 runs.

An individual batsman did well to receive thirty balls an hour. If he scored off, say, half of those, he'd have 20 runs in an hour, or 30 in a session. We felt obliged to slow things down as well. If that was their game, why should we increase the tempo?

We completely outplayed them in the First and Third Tests. They could have saved both of those games, but lacked the experience. At Kandy we left them 240 to win in two and a half hours plus twenty overs. After twenty-seven overs, they were bowled out for under a hundred. They didn't know how to play out time and continued going for their shots after the loss of early wickets. In the Third Test, they faced a deficit of 209 on first innings, but eventually had seven hours to bat out time on a placid pitch and play themselves into a match-saving position. Instead, they were bowled out for less than 150, giving us victory by an innings and 70 with three hours play to spare.

In the Second Test, we allowed them to get into a winning position. We dismissed them for 174 but they hit back well to bowl us out for 198. Our last five wickets went for 30 runs. I snapped up a couple of quick wickets before they got their noses ahead. Then Roy Dias made a century and Sidath Wettimuny 65, enabling Mendis to declare and leave us 266 to win in four and a half hours plus twenty overs. We'd dropped both players before they reached double figures. Had those catches been held, we'd have won in four days. As it was, we batted out time after being 10−2. Martin Crowe batted four hours for 19 and John Wright four and a half hours for 40-plus. We showed them how not to lose a match. In all, we batted for 86 overs and scored 123−4.

The Sri Lankans didn't play the game hard enough. They weren't mean. Until they learn that, I don't think they'll do themselves justice. Their batting was the main problem. They never got off to a good start and were invariably 20−2. Apart from Ranjan Madugalle, no-one got his head down for long periods. He was their outstanding batsman, though he was wasted at number six. He was the only one equipped to deal with myself and should have been moved up to three. Dias had injury problems. Had he been fit for all three Tests, things might have been different. His century in Colombo was a very good one even though he did enjoy a good deal of luck. Once Madugalle was out however, the tail was exposed. Only twice did they progress beyond 200.

Vinoodhan John was the pick of the bowlers. He created problems for all the batsmen and his return of sixteen wickets in the series was excellent. D. S. De Silva, their forty-two-year-old leg spinner bowled accurately, but didn't pose many problems. The Sri Lankans will have been disappointed with their overall performance, especially after beating us in England. Individually, they have some very talented players, but too many of them lack the discipline required to survive at Test level.

We were obviously delighted with our results. Our bowlers did a marvellous job in trying conditions. The Third Test was near-perfect. Our batsmen started to click and play long innings. John Reid's 180 in ten and a half hours was an example of how to overcome the heat and maintain concentration despite the distractions around him.

The standard of umpiring left something to be desired. It was barely satisfactory though, to be fair, they lacked experience at Test level.

Generally, their decision-making was acceptable and they responded well to enormous pressure in the Second Test when Sri Lanka were trying to bowl us out to win the match. One of the umpires from that Test was supposed to have stood in the last Test as well but was unaccountably removed. I suspect it was because he hadn't given Wright out caught behind in our backs-to-the-wall second innings. That was a great shame. I thought he was the most consistent umpire of the lot.

Most of the officials tended to over-react to certain situations. For instance, it was obvious that the home batsmen struggled against the short ball. Two of the umpires were indecently quick to protect them and order me not to bowl short of a length. In the First Test I bowled a bouncer to John. The umpire turned to me and said: 'You can't do that.' The next ball was about waist high and wide of the off stump. He called 'no-ball' for intimidatory bowling. Throughout the series, they had to be reminded that we were playing TEST cricket, not club cricket.

The umpires lost the respect of the players by getting upset over trifling matters and failing to defuse what could have been explosive situations. Believe it or not, one of them threw his hat on the ground in annoyance after John Bracewell had shown his disappointment at a bat-pad decision which went against him. The umpires took ages getting to their positions behind the stumps. To save time, I left my sun hat on the ground for one official to put in his pocket when he arrived. I then marched back to my mark ready to bowl. The umpire refused to pick up the hat, demanding that I give it to him personally. Play was interrupted while Geoff Howarth queried the decision. Finally, the umpire backed down.

The tour was a personal triumph for me. It allowed me to play in my fiftieth Test (and to take ten wickets in the match); to set a New Zealand record of 23 victims and take the 'Man of the Series' award which meant so much. My only disappointment was with the bat. I scored 75 runs in four innings. It still leaves me 180 runs short of the 2,000 target I'm aiming for to become the sixth player to achieve the 'double' double. Hopefully that milestone will be reached at home against the Pakistanis.

I'd like to pay a special tribute to Chandra Perrera, our liaison man. He was a true gentleman and did everything possible to make our stay on the Sacred Island as enjoyable as possible.

The Board of Control for cricket in Sri Lanka can be well satisfied with their efforts to make the series a success. The country is very capable of holding Test series in the future. With a few improvements here and there, I believe it could become a successful and challenging tour.

11

In Defence Of Overseas Cricketers

When he was Chairman of Selectors, Alec Bedser would frequently throw up his hands in despair at the quantity of overseas cricketers dominating the English averages. Bedser believed in the old maxim that the averages were the best barometer of up-and-coming talent. Yet he was confronted year after year with grand old Anglo-Saxon names like Alvin Kallicharran, Zaheer Abbas and Imran Khan! Add to those Barry Richards, Viv Richards, Gordon Greenidge, Richard Hadlee, Clive Rice, Mike Procter, Ken McEwan, Vincent van der Bijl and others and you begin to understand Bedser's frustration.

Picking an England tour party had become largely a shot in the dark. Some candidates barely had a century to their name, few bowlers had ever aspired to 100 wickets in a season. Whose fault was it—the game's administrators for allowing so many foreign cricketers onto English shores, or English cricketers themselves for not developing their own talents? It was and still is a commonly held view that filling the major domestic batting and bowling places with overseas stars stunts the growth of home-grown youngsters. It's a view Hadlee flatly rejects:

Without overseas players, the English county game would be dead. That may be hard for some people to swallow, but that's the way I see it. Sure, years ago when Warwickshire had half a dozen West Indians in the side, you could argue that it was detrimental to the development of the English game. Now the number has been limited to two players per county, that's fair and reasonable. Some teams have only one overseas player and I think they're placed at a disadvantage. People want to see the top names in the world and why shouldn't they? The game needs people to come and watch. It strikes me as a simple old formula . . . give them the best and they'll pay to see it.

I don't believe that it's a bad thing for English cricketers to be playing with and against international stars. Their own standards must improve for them to survive in the game. They must learn or perish. If they perish, they can't have been very good in the first place.

The success of Middlesex in recent seasons has been inspired by overseas players like Gomes, van der Bijl, Thomson and Daniel. That hasn't stopped the club providing a rich seam of talent for England. In fact, I believe it encouraged the development of players like Gatting, Emburey, Edmonds, Cowans and Downton. The same could be said of Somerset who've enjoyed unheard-of success with Richards and Garner in the side. It has given cricket lovers of that county something to watch and enjoy, and has put money into the coffers. I wonder if Botham would have emerged so dramatically if it hadn't been for the spirit created at Taunton?

Davison, Clift and, more recently, Andy Roberts have done an awful lot for Leicestershire too. Yet they still boast many fine young cricketers like Gower, Cook, Butcher and Garnham, all of whom have enriched the quality of local talent.

On the other side of the coin, Yorkshire have been going through a barren period. They're the only county club which refuses to introduce overseas players. What good has it done them?

I accept that two overseas players to each county means that two local players are kept out of the side, but it's only the inferior players who are kept out, not the best. Younger players are kept on the books for a year or so as apprentices with the second team, then, as they learn and improve, they'll get their chance either because their form demands it, or through injury to a senior pro. That's the way it has always been and there's as much opportunity for the youngster now as there ever was.

I don't think I'm keeping anyone out of the Notts team who's good enough to be playing first-class cricket. In their case, it'll be some time before the younger bowlers become reliable, consistent performers. They learn to do that, hopefully in the second eleven, with the occasional outing in the first team. Surely the fact that I am operating at one end with an English player like Kevin Saxelby or Kevin Cooper at the other is a good thing for them.

I feel that not enough English youngsters take advantage of a situation like that. They seem curiously reluctant to learn from the best players in the world. In the seven years I've had at Notts for instance, only one or two players have sat down for a serious discussion about bowling. The others have just coasted through.

It was a long time before Kevin Saxelby and I had a chat. I was willing to pass on any advice or help, but he seemed wary of me as though I was some sort of threat. Hopefully over the years at Trent Bridge, some of the young bowlers have learned something from watching, but I'm astonished that so few have asked. Perhaps they are in awe of me but there's no need to be. When you've been on the staff for seven years, you like to think you're one of the boys. I can appreciate a little reluctance, but over a beer at the end of the day or during those long periods of idleness, I'd have thought I was an easy enough guy to talk to. I don't really think it's my place to say 'do this' and 'do that' because they could easily resent it. It has to come from them. They shouldn't think that because I'm a Test player they would get a negative reaction.

This reticence is apparent, not just with me and Clive Rice, but with many overseas players. Perhaps that's why there's such an alarming amount of mediocrity in English cricket. A lot of very average players are making their living out of the game when really they shouldn't be in it . . . they should choose another career if that's their attitude. Those who choose professional sport are entertainers. It's show business. They're being paid to perform on a stage, and those who dig into their pockets to pay the wages deserve to see the best.

That means every day, not occasionally.

Where I play in Notts, we draw a lot of support from working-class folk who haven't a lot of cash to spare. There are plenty who don't have a job at all. Then there are the miners. Whatever political view you take of the strike, the fact remains that it's a dirty, dangerous and extremely uncomfortable job. Those guys underground deserve to relax in the sunshine and enjoy some top-class cricket in return for their money. Too often they don't get it.

Some of the 'shirkers' as I call them don't get away with it for long because their contracts are terminated. Unfortunately, there are a few others who do just enough to scrape through—limping to 1,000 runs in the year if they're batsmen, or contenting themselves with 50-60 wickets as bowlers. There are very few matchwinners among them.

Obviously not everyone can win matches. Alongside the stars you have to have a certain amount of bread-and-butter players who will chip in with 2—40 off twenty overs or collect 30-odd quick runs when they're needed. But there are days when those players have to do better than that. At Notts, Kevin Cooper's a good example. He'll do extremely valuable work supporting Saxelby or myself at the other end, but is quite capable of winning a game with a performance like his 8—44 which destroyed Middlesex.

I regard it as the duty of an overseas player to help draw the best out of those around him—to notice the players who are happy to coast along and spur them on to greater effort by giving them targets to aim at. Clive is a great exponent of that. Before the season starts, he gives every member of the team a target to match their ability. Look what happened: Chris Broad played for England; Eddie Hemmings was unlucky not to be chosen after winning international recognition late in his career; Bruce French broke the club's wicket-keeping record, was voted keeper of the year, and rightly got picked for the India tour; and Tim Robinson earned a place on the tour as well.

As an overseas player, I have to put up with a certain amount of abuse and poisonous letters. One chap threatened to scar me for life if I didn't stop bowling bouncers at Geoff Boycott—that one was put in the hands of the police—and there are several each year telling me to go home. There are just as many flattering letters though. I guess those people recognise what I've always maintained — that the overseas star has a lot to offer and that the day he is banished, English cricket will suffer. He's the one who will set a game alight. By the same token, we have a lot to gain from being in England, and I don't just mean financially. I learned more in my first six weeks in 1978 than I had in the previous six years!

There's an argument that too much of a good thing can be dangerous. I don't hold with that either. Spectators will never get bored with seeing the best in the world performing on the daily circuit and I don't believe it lessens their appetite for Test cricket. They look forward to a Viv Richards/Ian Botham or a Richard Hadlee/Derek Randall clash. It creates another aspect to the game which wouldn't arise otherwise. Similarly when Botham and I are playing against each other, there's that extra bit of excitement, that extra selling factor.

It's probably true that other countries have benefitted from having so many of their players getting used to English conditions. I couldn't deny that the West Indies for example now feel just as much at home on English pitches as England themselves . . . more so judging by the results of the 1984 summer! The English seam and swing bowlers are possibly less likely to trouble batsmen like Richards, Greenidge and Lloyd who play in England every summer. In addition, Joel Garner and Malcolm Marshall have grown up with English wickets and don't have any problem adapting when they play a Test series. The same applies to me. Equally, England players have enjoyed the experience of batting and bowling against the world's best on a regular basis, so the surprise element has been cancelled out for them too.

Then what about Sri Lanka? None of their players are used to English conditions and yet they come over for one Test Match and perform superbly. It boils down to professionalism. Whatever the conditions, you still have to perform on a given day when literally anything can happen. In my case, it wasn't a very appealing prospect when New Zealand toured Sri Lanka early in 1984. Yet I came away

115

with 23 wickets in three Tests and an average of 10 — quite unbelievable.

What I'm saying is that I adapted to foreign conditions where the ball was swinging. I realised I had to bowl a fuller length to get success. Any cricketer worth his salt can adapt to any conditions. Those in England are the fairest of all. Australian pitches are very hard on the feet and legs but the unfairest pitches in the world are in India and Pakistan. They are completely foreign to white teams. The black countries, West Indies, India, Pakistan and Sri Lanka would all find it easier adapting to English or New Zealand conditions than we would to theirs.

Summing it up, I would say that the benefits of overseas players in England far outweigh the disadvantages. Those who claim otherwise are kidding themselves. It's no good pointing at us when looking for an excuse for England's poor performances at Test level in recent years. The fact is that the standard of English cricket has slipped while the rest of the world has caught up or forged ahead. It comes and goes in cycles.

12

The Final Push

The double was a formality by mid-August. Hadlee's run target came down by half when he scored 51 and 10 at Folkestone five days after the unbeaten 210. He bagged five more wickets in the match, leaving 7 for the 100. Disappointingly, Notts were slipping behind in the title race. They gathered only six points from the draw with Kent but at least had the satisfaction of seeing Paul Johnson (surely a name for the future) reach the highest score of his short career, 133. And a brief word about the skipper. Rice was heading for a repeat of Hadlee's double century when he declared the innings with his personal score 152 not out!

Overnight it was the long haul from the south coast to Blackpool on the north-west coast for the match with Lancashire, one of the bottom clubs in the table. With 59 runs and 7 wickets required, Hadlee was in a position to make history there and then.

This was the twentieth match and it would have been very satisfying to complete the double within my budgeted number of games. I thought I was going to do it when I came in to bat at 174—4. I started blitzing the ball all over the place and was fairly unlucky to get out on 38. I got a full length delivery from Watkinson and shovelled it out from around my foot, only to be caught at mid-wicket. So the chance was gone and I was 21 runs short. The match was still a landmark though because I collected my 100th wicket of the season—just.

I'd taken two wickets in the Lancashire first innings, leaving me on 95. By the time the second innings came around, the pitch was a real feather bed – low, slow, just what I didn't want. I couldn't see myself getting any more wickets. Not only was the pitch dead, but the ball was in tatters when I opened the bowling again. I knocked over Alan Ormrod's castle that night and Lancashire were 30 – 1 at stumps. Next morning, I had Chadwick taken at cover by Randall (97) and Folley exactly the same way (98). Watkinson was hanging around. He'd scored 61. The wickets had come with me bowling around the wicket. Bowling over allowed me no variation. The batsmen could just play themselves in. Throughout the season I picked up a lot of wickets bowling around.

It didn't seem to be working with Watkinson and I was getting a little fed up. I decided to bowl him a series of short ones which came up about waist high. Then I dug one in a bit more, got some extra lift and he tried to pull me. The ball flew off the top edge and presented me with a nice caught and bowled. One to go, but Lancashire were down to their last pair, Maynard and the Jamaican, Les McFarlane.

Les doesn't have a great batting record, but I had only two balls to finish the over, knowing full well that Eddie Hemmings would probably get him if I didn't. Well, Eddie didn't and I had another go at the number eleven. As I've said earlier, bowling at tailenders isn't my favourite pastime. I went round the wicket again to change the angle and sure enough, his off stump came flying out of the ground. That was it – 100 wickets and what a great sight. They all came round to congratulate me and gave me the ball. I've got it mounted at home.

Since we only wanted 64 to win, there wasn't much chance of getting the final, 21 runs. In many ways I was glad, because I really wanted to complete the double at Trent Bridge in front of our own supporters. All this time, we were closing on Essex. It promised to be one of the most exciting finishes to the season in recent years.

And so to Trent Bridge, for match number twenty-one against Warwickshire during the August Bank Holiday.

118

*Rice won the toss and put Warwickshire in, as was his
wont. Notts didn't distinguish themselves in the field on the
Saturday and Warwickshire reached a reasonable total of
261. Hadlee suffered as much as any bowler, but was in
superb form. Only Amiss and Humpage had any answer
to him, and he finished with one of his best analyses of
the season: 26.2 overs, 9 maidens, 6—55.*

*Trent Bridge was bathed in sunshine on the Bank Holiday
Monday, and a crowd of around 3000 had gathered to
watch Hadlee complete the formalities. He had to wait for
a second wicket partnership of 178 between Robinson and
Randall. Hadlee takes up the story:*

We often lost a wicket five or ten minutes before lunch. While
Randall and Robinson were batting, Clive asked me if I
fancied going in next to get the suspense over with. I said
I preferred to wait till after lunch. Within moments, Robinson
was out to keep up that peculiar record of ours. Clive went
in at four and my turn came after the break when Randall
was caught behind off Gladstone Small.

As I walked down the pavilion steps past the members,
there was a buzz around the whole ground. They all knew
how many I wanted. The scene was ripe for something to
happen—sunshine, plenty of spectators and the target in sight.
On the way to the middle, a rare negative thought forced
its way into my mind. What a disaster if I failed in front of
all these people! It was contrary to everything I'd been
conditioning myself to do and I knew I had to dismiss it fast.
The best way was to get off the mark. I nudged a couple
of singles and that eased the tension.

Geoff Humpage, the Warwickshire keeper said: 'Two
down, 19 to go.' He was aware of the last detail, as was the
whole Warwickshire team. There was no way they would
give me anything. Chris Old was bowling. He overpitched
one ball and I whacked it back over his head for four. That
got me going. Then I clobbered a 6 and another 4 and with
a single in there somewhere, I was on 17. One hit would
do it. Old pitched one up again, just short of a length. It had
to be a slog shot. I dragged the ball wide of mid-on, well
clear of the field for 4 and I had the double!

The crowd at the Radcliffe Road end gave me a standing ovation; the public address system made the official announcement and members came out to congratulate me. It was just a very nice occasion and a great sense of relief.

The news travelled fast. Hadlee was one of the first to break it to his adoring public in New Zealand. One local writer reported that: 'Hadlee was acclaimed as the greatest all-round cricketer in the game today.' Is that right?

The bare facts are that he scored 1179 runs (average 51.26) and took 117 wickets (average 14.05) in twenty-one matches. Fred Titmus in 1967 took twenty-five games to score 1096 runs and take 106 wickets. The double was an old cricketing landmark that any half-decent all-rounder would regard as the minimum requirement to confirm his status. Against that, the general standard of cricket is undoubtedly much higher now than it was between the wars or in the early 1900's when George Hirst did his 2000 runs/200 wickets double. In other words, there are probably fewer 'rabbits' available to the bowler. As well, few of those double achievers were main strike bowlers for their countries and counties as Hadlee was.

It's interesting to consider the number of world class players who failed to achieve the double. The great Gary Sobers had three go's in 1969, 70 and 71 when he was captain of Notts. Frankly, he didn't come anywhere near. His best effort was in 1970 with 1742 runs and 64 wickets. Mike Procter tried for season after season. He too managed the runs but not the wickets. His best haul was 81. It sounds close, but 19 wickets can still take a lot of getting. Taking Hadlee's budget as a basis, Procter was almost four matches away. Mushtaq enjoyed a vintage season in 1969 and again in 1972 when his run aggregates of 1831 and 1949 still stand as the highest of any all-rounder since the championship 'shrank' in 1969. However, the Pakistani leg-spinner never got beyond 78 wickets in a season.

What of Botham? He can always point to Test match interference. Play one Test and you're likely to miss two county games. His best effort was in 1982 when Pakistan were the tourists. Botham had 1241 runs and 66 wickets.

Soulbrothers. Hadlee and Clive Rice take time off to watch Nottingham Forest as often as possible

Exposed! Rival and hero in a rare moment of togetherness

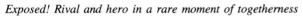

Geoff Boycott — 'the hardest guy I've ever bowled to'

'I should have taken my batting more seriously'

'Allan Lamb who is about as English as me!'

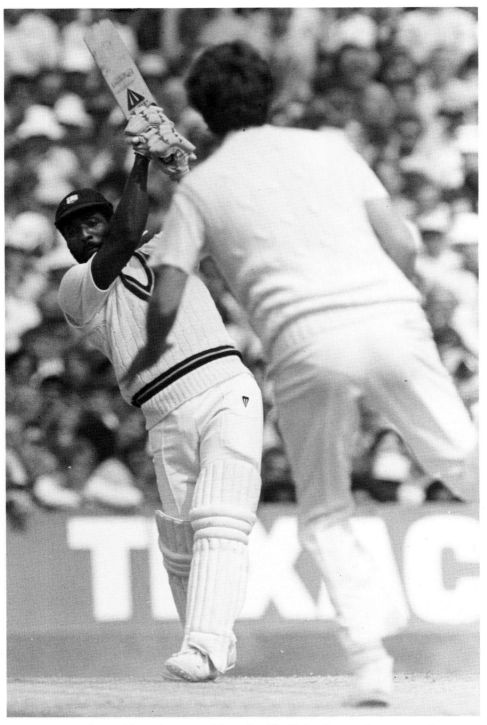

'No batsman in the world worries me unduly — but Viv Richards can take you apart'

'Who's the best all-rounder in the world? Clive Rice wins the trophy, Kapil Dev comes second —
but Ian Botham's record won't be·beaten'

'An understanding wife is essential. Thank goodness Karen played cricket herself!'

'I love getting back to the homestead after a long, hard summer in England'

'Time to relax with Nicholas. These moments are precious'

If the cap fits, wear it! Nicholas Hadlee showing he could be a chip off the old block

Zaheer gets the Hadlee treatment. 'Bowling is my greatest joy'

It is debatable how seriously Botham ever took the double challenge, if, indeed, he ever gave it a second thought. With his remarkable Test record, it probably seemed small beer.

Imran Khan could never mount a realistic challenge despite several attempts. The runs came, but 65 wickets was his best effort in 1976. Tony Greig was another failed 'doubler'. His best performance in 1971 left him 23 wickets adrift—five matches by Hadlee's calculations. Keith Boyce was the closest of all in 1972. The West Indian all-rounder scored 1023 runs and took 82 wickets.

Hadlee's captain, Clive Rice was considered by many to be the finest all-rounder in the world until a neck injury virtually ruled him out of full-time bowling in 1982. By his own admission, he tried 'like hell' to achieve the target. Notts' title-winning season of 1981 offered him the best and, as it turned out, the last chance. His 1,462 runs were backed up with only 65 wickets.

By modern standards, a wicket haul of 65 upwards is good going. The double can never again be taken for granted. Even with the advantage of good weather, it must be considered a major achievement. One should not forget that there were several other international all-rounders who could have taken advantage of the summer the way Hadlee did. The two England spinners, Vic Marks and Geoff Miller missed the chance, albeit fairly narrowly. They may never get a better opportunity. Marks had 1262 runs and 86 wickets; Miller 933 runs and 87 wickets.

Who else is capable of the double? Over to Hadlee:

I can't really see anyone unless it's Miller or Marks. Kapil Dev will never do it—he won't get the wickets; Imran would probably be the same, although he tells me if he returns to English cricket, he intends to shorten his run the way I did. Malcolm Marshall should get the wickets alright, but I doubt he'd get the runs. Then I suppose Phil Edmonds and Peter Willey have got to have an outside chance, though I honestly don't think so.

It's hard to imagine what it takes out of you over a season. Apart from the work load, there's the pressure of trying to reach a target. That's why spinners ought to stand a better chance. They can bowl 700 overs a season without putting their bodies under such strain.

Titmus was quick to acknowledge Hadlee's achievement though he says he grew a little tired of people stopping him in the street and telling him that Hadlee had broken his record! There was no record to break!

'Hadlee's a super cricketer and I wholeheartedly congratulate him. He is by far the best bowler of the world's top all-rounders. Now he's proved that the batting side of his game is top class as well. It should be an example to others now. Hadlee's proved that the double's not out of the question and let's hope it encourages others to strive that bit harder.

'To me it was always important, but then I wouldn't have been much of a cricketer if I hadn't managed 1000 runs and 100 wickets in our seasons. To be honest, I always used to make bloomin' sure I played against Oxford and Cambridge. They were better in those days than they are now, but it was still a good opportunity to get a few statistics under your belt. Credit to Hadlee for missing out those games and still making it.

'Another thing people forget is that wickets these days are generally slower than in my day. A bowler has to put so much more in to get anything out. There are too many stalemate wickets in my view. The ball hardly bounces and you often see off-spinners operating without a slip. That was unheard of when I was playing!

'I think all medium-pace bowlers should take a close look at Hadlee. From the very first ball he delivers, he's straight on the spot. A medium-pacer should be able to bowl straight all day long, but sadly, too few of them do.'*

Hadlee was delighted with the improvement in his batting:

I'd always had a weakness against spin, preferring to slog them instead of playing them properly. That was the typical approach of a bowler who 'did a bit of batting'. Now I have a higher regard for my ability with the bat. Last season I played spin bowling better than at any stage of my career. I was picking the one to hit. The confidence I gained from that was unbelievable. Spinners didn't get me out very often during the double campaign.

Most of the time I got myself out. Out of 33 innings, I was bowled once, not out 8 times, and caught on 22 occasions. Those catches were usually miscues from taking risks, holing out to cover or long-off or deep mid wicket.

The season was far from over for Notts. Middlesex held Essex to a draw and Rice's team were suddenly back in with a chance. Keith Fletcher launched a stinging attack on his Middlesex counterpart, Mike Gatting for not accepting his challenge and for killing the game stone dead. The pendulum seemed to be swinging back towards Notts. Victory over Northants at Trent Bridge left them a single point behind Essex—with a game in hand!

Broad, back from his Test match blitzing at the hands of Marshall, Holding and Garner, hit 94 before lunch on the first day. Randall was out cheaply, but Robinson progressed to 86 before David Steele had him leg before. Rice was building up a steady score when Hadlee joined him on 252 – 4. The pressure was off and Hadlee started to enjoy himself. Here's Rice's account:

'Richard was going like a train and heading for the fastest hundred of the season. At the other end, I was like a carthorse in comparison. At tea, he was 74 not out and I told him to pull his finger out and go for the fastest ton of the season.

'He objected, saying it wasn't in the interest of the team. I told him not to be such a silly bugger. I'd stick around and make sure of a solid score . . . he was free to go for it. We worked out that he had 15 minutes after tea to beat Mike Gatting's record. He already had the double and the fastest televised Sunday League 50, so he might as well go for the lot.

'Four runs later, Hadlee took a huge swing at Steele and was caught on the boundary for 78.

Bitter disappointment followed at Hove where Notts came up against a resolute Sussex batting display. Parker gained some revenge for the buffeting he took off Hadlee at Trent Bridge, by making 101 in the Sussex total of 436. The game

123

finished with Notts chasing 278 for victory in about thirty-five overs on the last day. It was never on. Still they were enjoying their position at the top of the table. It was the first time all season they'd actually climbed into number one spot. It lasted all too briefly. Essex beat Lancashire in two days in their last match of the season. Everything rested on Notts' final fixture at Taunton on 8 September. Victory would give them their second championship title in four years.

In the meantime, Hadlee was being showered with gifts and awards everywhere he went. His colleague Tim Robinson said:

'It seemed that someone was arriving at the dressing room every five minutes with a crate of champagne for him. I've never seen so many prizes showered on one person. Sir Robert Muldoon, the former New Zealand prime minister also sent a cable, and messages arrived from all over New Zealand.'

Hadlee won three Cricketer of the Week awards along with several Bowler of the Month trophies. He was up to his eyes in cases of sherry and champagne, neither of which he particularly enjoys. Notts awarded him a Capo di Monte statuette; club supporters produced trophies of various descriptions, and a pensioner sent him a pair of gold cufflinks.

Possibly his most treasured 'prize' however was a £600 gold medallion from his New Zealand sponsors, Leopard Breweries. On it were inscribed the details of the double achievement. The medallion was presented by Brian Clough, the Nottingham Forest manager for whom Hadlee has a great admiration:

That was my Olympic Gold Medal. The satisfaction of achieving a place in the history books was enough in itself, but I must admit that I do enjoy winning titles and awards. It proves that I am successful.

That's a philosophy which, for a long time, his manager, Ken Taylor couldn't grasp:

'I didn't understand Richard. To me he was always a

124

magnificent cricketer and I accepted him as that. He felt other people didn't realise his worth, so he had to keep offering them tangible proof. I assumed he was confident of his own ability and reputation, but I don't think he was. If it had been me I wouldn't have given a damn about other people.

'Over the years I've thought about it a lot. Now I think I agree with Richard's attitude towards awards. In Nottingham we have the Home Brewery awards. They're given to the outstanding capped and uncapped players at the club each month. The problem is that Richard always wins it. There've been mutterings about how idiotic it is, but Hadlee's view is that it's up to the others to take the title from him. He's right. If he's the best player, he should have the prize'.

Did Hadlee feel that reaching the double proved that he was the best all-rounder in the game?

That's not for me to say. I'm pleased to be in that class with Imran, Kapil and Botham though no-one will ever surpass Gary Sobers. Then there were players like Trevor Bailey, Keith Miller and Tony Greig at his best. It's nice to be remembered as one of a small, select band.

I'll never be the best of all-time—I've spent too many years batting down the order. But, over the years I hope I've done enough to be considered one of the best all rounders New Zealand has produced.

For the record, Hadlee also came within one run of the Sunday League 'double' of 400 runs and 20 wickets. If he'd realised there was such a target, he'd have reached it.

There wasn't a moment's respite for Hadlee or his hard-pressed captain, Rice. They travelled to Taunton early in September with a double mission—to beat Ian Botham's Somerset and take the title, and to pit their considerable wits against each other in the Silk Cut Challenge, a competition to find the unofficial best all-rounder in the world.

First things first. Notts were without Kevin Saxelby and Peter Such for the most important match of the last three years. They were still bothered by injury. Young Andy Pick and the veteran Mike Bore stepped into the breach. On

Saturday, 8 September, Botham won the toss and decided to bat. The weather was intermittently sunny and cool with the prospect of showers. Hadlee soon had Nigel Felton back in the pavilion, caught by French without scoring. Nigel Popplewell followed in the same way, but Peter Roebuck and Hadlee's New Zealand colleague, Martin Crowe put on 68 for the third wicket. It was Crowe's first season in English cricket and he had every reason to be pleased with it.

Crowe made 57 and Jeremy Lloyds 94 in the Somerset total of 274. A couple of hours had been lost to rain on Saturday, but Notts collected maximum bowling bonus points on the Monday. Hadlee took his eleventh bag of four wickets in an innings and Kevin Cooper also had a haul of four. French continued his remarkable season with six catches behind the wicket — a performance which was soon to be rewarded with a place on the England tour.

Rice declared the Notts first innings at 222−7 off 65.3 overs, knowing that a result was all that mattered. Batting bonus points were now irrelevant. Broad was in good shape, hitting 88 and Randall was run out for 64. At the close, Somerset were 32−0 in reply.

On the last day, heavy drizzle in the Bristol area somehow managed to stop short of Taunton, but the threat of rain lingered for most of the morning. Television cameras had arrived to record what could be a tremendous climax to the season. Botham was in an invidious position. He had to be seen to be fair to everyone in his declaration. If he left Notts a generous target, Essex would feel aggrieved; if the target was out of reach, he would be held responsible for killing the spectacle. He had the perfect answer: 'I'm not interested in Notts or Essex, only Somerset!'

In the event, Botham set Notts 297 to win in 60 overs. More fine batting by Roebuck and Lloyds had enabled him to declare the second innings closed at 244−5. The wicket was taking spin now. Eddie Hemmings had claimed four of the five wickets, though some of Rice's field placings had the spectators wondering about his tactics. He kept several close fielders up, allowing Lloyds and Crowe to

126

hit boundaries almost at will. The target seemed a stiff one, but it was still tantalisingly within reach. The weather had improved and on a pleasantly warm late summer afternoon, an enraptured audience prepared for the dénouement.

They would be privileged to see one of the most exciting day's cricket in the history of the competition. Over to Hadlee:

Botham got it just about right, though he certainly wasn't doing us any favours. If we wanted that title, we had to go for it all the way. Someone had to get a century or damn near to it.

Broad and Robinson made a fine start with 70 for the first wicket. Broad had made 45 of them when he was first out shortly after tea. The England opener felt he'd anchored his back foot when going forward to Vic Marks, but was given out, stumped by Trevor Gard. In the next over, Robinson played back to the left arm spinner, Steve Booth, missed the turn, and was bowled. The innings lost momentum and the five-an-over run rate was slipping behind.

Randall soon followed when, on 14, he drove a low return catch to Marks. That was 92—3 in the 29th over. Paul Johnson looked the part and hit beautifully through the offside. With Rice taking his time at the other end, Johnson made 21 before charging down the wicket to Marks and falling to an easy stumping chance. The score —136—4. The target now was 138 in the remaining 20 overs—a rate of almost 7 an over and going up all the time. The onus was on Rice and Hadlee, as it always seemed fated to be. As long as that pair was together, anything could happen.

Rice had taken nine overs to score his first eight runs. Now he took charge. Making use of the shorter boundary behind Booth's end, Rice drove mercilessly over the top and pulled anything remotely short of a length for 4. His half century came up in 64 minutes, but more importantly, he and Hadlee had put on 53 in eight overs to swing the game around in Notts' favour once more. Hadlee was beginning to time the ball nicely now, but when the left

127

*hander had cut and pulled his way to 28 in double quick
time, he was out, controversially:*

I went for a big hit off the left arm spinner but the ball seemed
to hang in the air over the mid-wicket boundry. Jeremy
Lloyds caught it, but crashed into the advertising boards as
he did so. Many people thought it was 6. I had some doubt
and waited for the umpires to decide. They had no hesitation
in giving me out. You could say I was robbed by the Somerset
commercial manager! If there'd been the usual rope instead
of a board, the shot would have been a 6. With a board, the
ball had to clear it completely to be deemed a boundary. The
fielder was allowed to touch the fence as he made the catch,
and even catch the ball over the fence. We were a bit unlucky.

The Nottingham Evening Post *took a much stronger line:
'There must have been millions of people who watched the
incident on television . . . and thought it unfair that a man
should be given out when the fielder clearly rebounds off an
advertising board. And they would have been right to think
that way. . . Under law 32, the catch was perfectly fair . . .
What a law! And when a championship may have been
decided by it, it's a bad, bad law. It should either be amended
or scrapped altogether!'*

*Hadlee's dismissal was one of the game's turning points.
Keith Fletcher, the Essex captain, was listening to reports
on the game from his county headquarters at Chelmsford.
In his mind, it had swung back again, though there was
still the problem of Rice.*

*With support from French, the captain took the game
by the scruff of the neck, blasting his way to 98 in 109
balls. The title was back in sight until Marks bowled a full
toss and Rice over-reacted. What should have been a
certain boundary claimed his wicket. He caught the ball
on the splice and it lobbed gently to the substitute fielder
Richard Ollis standing some way in from the fence. Rice
was mortified, Notts were 39 runs short. Furious with
himself, the skipper virtually threw his bat away at the steps
to the dressing room, dived inside and lay prostrate on
the seat, bathed in sweat. He couldn't bear to watch the
end. Only once did he get up from his makeshift 'bed' and*

that was to see French get out. For the rest of the innings he relied on Hadlee's running commentary.

Hemmings and Cooper went with only 2 runs added. As Fletcher and his Essex team mates prepared to celebrate 200 miles away, and Notts supporters resigned themselves to the inevitable, thirty-seven-year-old Mike Bore walked out practically unnoticed for his second championship innings of the season. These days, the Yorkshireman spent most of his time captaining the Colts team and coaching youngsters at the indoor nets. With two overs to go, the target was 27 and few gave Notts a prayer. Bore waged such an assault on Marks and Booth who bowled unchanged for most of the innings, that Notts came within spitting distance of their second title in four years. Fourteen were needed from the last over.

Bore hit Booth's first and second balls for four then wisely turned the third for two. Four were required off the last three balls of the season. Bore wasn't going to be panicked. One hit would do it. He blocked the fourth ball then decided to attack the fifth. The batsman aimed to strike it over long-off, but Ollis took the catch three yards inside the boundary. It was all over. Notts had lost the match and the championship by four runs! Fletcher danced with joy in Chelmsford, Rice was inconsolable in Taunton. He said: 'I'm 35 but today I feel 50. I was shattered to come so near and lose. All that hard work and I go and give it away by holing out to a full toss. I should have hit the ball out of Somerset! The match was in my control and I let it slip. Full marks to Mike Bore for his heroics. I couldn't bear to watch them I'm afraid.'

Botham strode past the gaggle of radio reporters, television cameramen and photographers to congratulate Rice on his team's effort. The Notts captain, his hair plastered to his head, looked dazed and exhausted. Says Hadlee:

I've never seen him like that before. He was absolutely drained. The title meant so much to him, as it did to all of us. It was incredible that it should be decided off the last-but-one ball of the last over of the last day of the season.

SOMERSET v NOTTINGHAMSHIRE
24th Championship match

Played at Taunton, September 8, 10, and 11, 1984
Somerset (22pts) beat Notts (6pts) by 3 runs.

SOMERSET

	First Innings		Second Innings	
1. P. M. Roebuck	c French b Hadlee	44	st French b Hemmings	78
2. N. A. Felton	c French b Hadlee	0	lbw Hemmings	15
3. N. F. Popplewell	c French b Hadlee	19	c and b Hemmings	9
4. M. D. Crowe	c French b Cooper	57	c Cooper b Hemmings	45
5. J. M. Lloyds	c French b Hemmings	94	not out	63
6. I. T. Botham	c French b Cooper	0		
7. V. J. Marks	c Hadlee b Cooper	22	not out	8
8. J. G. Wyatt	c Randall b Hadlee	5	st French b Bore	18
9. G. V. Palmer	b Cooper	19		
10. T. Gard	b Hemmings	0		
11. S. C. Booth	not out	0		
Extras		14		8
Total	(94.5 overs)	274	(5 wkts dec.)	244

BOWLERS:								
Hadlee	23	8	59	4	5	1	13	0
Pick	15	3	46	0	5	2	12	0
Rice	10	1	29	0				
Cooper	22.5	9	57	4	5	3	3	0
Hemmings	20	5	63	2	35	6	123	4
Bore	4	1	6	0	26	3	85	1

NOTTINGHAMSHIRE

	First Innings		Second Innings	
1. B. C. Broad	not out	88	st Gard b Marks	45
2. R. T. Robinson	lbw Crowe	4	b Booth	21
3. D. W. Randall	run out	64	c and b Marks	14
4. C. E. B. Rice	lbw Palmer	17	c sub b Marks	98
5. P. Johnson	st Gard b Booth	16	st Gard b Marks	21
6. R. J. Hadlee	c Roebuck b Marks	10	c Lloyds b Booth	28
7. B. N. French	c Lloyds b Marks	10	c Palmer b Marks	24
8. E. E. Hemmings	c and b Booth	5	st Gard b Booth	1
9. K. E. Cooper			st Gard b Marks	0
10. M. K. Bore			c sub b Booth	27
11. R. A. Pick			not out	4
Extras		8		10
Total	(7 wkts dec 65.3 overs)	222		293

BOWLERS:								
Botham	10	2	42	0	6	1	18	0
Crowe	12	1	34	1	2	0	16	0
Marks	22	4	64	2	27	0	111	6
Palmer	10	3	39	1				
Booth	10.3	1	30	2	24.5	2	138	4
Lloyds	1	0	5	0				

The funny thing is that Essex won the championship, but 1984 will be remembered more for the team which narrowly failed to take it from them.

Thanks to Mike Bore, we got closer than we deserved to beating Somerset. It wasn't really that defeat which cost us the title however. We should have beaten Derbyshire but let ourselves get bowled out for 136 in 35 overs. That cost us dearly. Kent were nine wickets down at Folkestone and we couldn't finish them off. Against Yorkshire near the start of the season, we needed 306 for victory, but fell six runs short. We didn't show the consistency needed to win the championship. Throughout the season we only held 65% of our catches. In my opinion Essex were the better team.

For us to finish second was a fair reflection of the season. Frankly, we weren't good enough championship material. Overall, though, it was an excellent season. Broad and Randall played for England; Robinson and French got selected for the India tour and I did the double in my best-ever season for the club. You can't complain at that.

Fletcher and his team retained the title, fourteen points ahead of Notts. The Essex captain said that last day had been the longest day of his life: 'I wasted more nervous energy listening to the bulletins than I ever do playing!' Here's how they finished.

Final Championship Table 1984

	P	W	L	D	T	Bat	Bwl	Pts
1 Essex (1)	24	13	3	8	0	64	83	355
2 Nottinghamshire (14)	24	12	3	9	0	68	81	341
3 Middlesex (2)	24	8	7	9	0	63	78	269
4 Leicestershire (4)	24	8	2	14	0	60	78	266
5 Kent (7)	24	8	3	11	2	45	65	254
6 Sussex (11)	24	7	6	10	1	54	79	249
7 Somerset (10)	24	6	7	11	0	60	78	234
8 Surrey (8)	24	6	6	12	0	62	72	230
9 Warwickshire (5)	24	6	7	11	0	71	60	227
10 Worcestershire (16)	24	5	5	14	0	66	74	220
11 Northants (6)	24	5	9	9	1	58	56	202
12 Derbyshire (9)	24	4	6	14	0	72	66	202
13 Glamorgan (15)	24	4	2	18	0	65	71	200
14 Yorkshire (17)	24	5	4	15	0	59	55	194
15 Hampshire (3)	24	3	13	8	0	58	62	168
16 Lancashire (12)	24	1	9	14	0	49	72	137
17 Gloucestershire (13)	24	1	10	13	0	58	61	135

13

Battle Of The Supermen

Our two heroes, Hadlee and Rice were ready for home.
Before they could jet away to the southern hemisphere,
they had one more important engagement in their diaries.
Just when you might have thought things would be winding
down, the pair had to wind themselves up for a unique
battle of wits and reputations.

Sports Sponsorship International were staging the
world's first all-rounder competition, feeding the public's
fascination for the 'Supermen' of cricket. It was a five-way
affair involving an Englishman, a West Indian, an Indian,
a New Zealander and a South African. No Australian
readily sprang to mind, though if Greg Chappell had not
retired, he'd have been an automatic choice. Imran Khan,
a cult figure since his heroic series in England, was
recovering from a long-standing injury.

After their exhausting season, a trial on television was
the last thing Hadlee and Rice needed. The money was
good though — £6,000 to the winner, scaling down to
£2,000 for the last man. Taunton was the 'circus ring' and
ITV's World of Sport gave the event maximum television
coverage. For them it was an important coup. Apart from
'Roses' or the occasional MCC match, ITV had been frozen
out of cricket by the BBC's monopoly.

Ian Botham, Malcolm Marshall, Kapil Dev, Richard
Hadlee and Clive Rice would each bat for sixteen overs
and bowl four overs at each of the opponents. The
batsman's score would be divided by the number of times

he was dismissed, then multiplied by the number of wickets
he took. If anyone failed to take a wicket, his score would
be zero . . . even 150 times 0 is 0! It was no great surprise
that Hadlee was the bookies' favourite at 9-4.

I was flattered but not very happy. Starting favourite put extra
pressure on me. It would have been much nicer to be an
underdog. The concept of the tournament was good, but the
formula left a lot to be desired. Clive had thought it out well
and publicly declared his intention to build a steady score
rather than a vast one, but without losing his wicket. He
figured that the risk of hitting out for a big total, only to have
it halved or quartered by a couple of unnecessary dismissals,
wasn't worth taking. Poor old Clive had a torrid time at the
crease. He played and missed several times, was dropped
once and got hit as well. He also played some superb shots
to finish on 73 not out. It was the lowest score of the day,
but, significantly, it was unbeaten.

Next man in was Marshall. What a nightmare he had! His
innings began pretty well and he reached 50 still intact. All
his ground work was shattered when Kapil Dev had him out
twice. Then, to everyone's amazement, including his own,
Rice knocked him over four more times in his first four overs
of the day. That included a hat-trick, not bad for a man with
a damaged shoulder who only bowled for Notts when there
was no-one else!

Marshall was effectively out of the competition, but more
importantly, Rice's total had already shot up to 292 (73 x
4) and he still had 12 overs left. Most of the others were
wicket-less and had used up half of their quota. Rice had
virtually won and at that early stage, the rest were playing
only for the minor positions.

Botham provided the batting highlight of the day although
he lost an early wicket with a needless run-out, and was
dismissed again next ball. That meant he really had to go
some. He showed his immense annoyance by hammering the
bowlers out of sight. Botham hit 10 sixes and 14 fours as
he powered his way to 163. Rice received more stick than
most, no fewer than 70 runs coming from his four over stint.
It made absolutely no difference to his position.

I got out twice quite early on, but made 149 with three sixes and 13 fours. My problem was that I didn't take a wicket all day. My batting average of 49.66 therefore was multiplied by zero which gave me a grand total of zero and fourth place! It seemed very strange to pick up 117 county wickets during the season, then on the day, to remain empty-handed. I had three catches dropped. Had they been held, my total would have shot up to around the 150 mark and put me in second place.

Kapil batted last and only he had a chance of overhauling Rice. If the Indian captain could reach 92 without loss, and if Rice failed to take any more wickets, Kapil would have won. However, Rice got him out twice, and Botham once. By surviving the last four overs, he did enough to secure the runner-up prize.

Rice took the £6,000, the silver cup and the crown of World's Greatest All-Rounder. The players would all agree however, that performances in Tests and first-class cricket were a fairer indication. On the day, we had to admit, Rice worked it out better than anyone else. We didn't talk much about it afterwards. I guess he thought it was diplomatic to stay silent! My county captain also got £1,000 for the best batting performance while Kapil took the £1,000 best bowling award.

Paul Downton and Bob Taylor were behind the stumps at different times, and county players from Worcester, Gloucestershire and Somerset did the fielding. Nigel Felton, the Somerset opener took £250 for best fielder.

We all agreed that the scoring system wasn't right. No-one minded getting punished as a batsman for losing one's wicket, but it seemed unfair that a bowler could give away as many runs as he liked and get off scot-free! Surely it's just as important to restrict runs as to take wickets. Rice conceded 186 runs from 16 overs, whereas Kapil only had 90 hit off him. Rice went unpunished for being expensive. It may be necessary next time to have the bowling average subtracted from the batting so that a plus or minus figure is arrived at. Under that scoring system, Rice would still have won, but with a smaller victory margin. The competition would have been closer and fairer.

134

I hear that Silk Cut are happy to continue the sponsorship for two to three years. If I'm invited again, I'll certainly be available. It was damned hard work, but the money was attractive and the honour of being world champ, even in slightly contrived conditions, made it worthwhile.

FINAL PLACINGS:

1. Clive Rice	73 runs × 7 wickets	511 pts	£6,000
2. Kapil Dev	117 runs (÷4) × 4 wickets	117 pts	£5,000
3. Ian Botham	163 runs (÷3) × 1 wicket	54 pts	£4,000
4. Richard Hadlee	149 runs (÷3) × 0	0 pts	£3,000
5. Malcolm Marshall	97 runs (÷7) × 0	0 pts	£2,000

14

A Question Of Loyalty?

Hadlee's views on his future reflect his business-like attitude to life and, to some people, are controversial:

When I retire from the Test scene, I may possibly play some cricket in South Africa. That could be in a couple of years time. It wouldn't be a political gesture, purely business. I've turned down several offers to play there, some of them recent. The first came from Northern Transvaal in 1981 when the bait dangled in front of me was 10,000 rand. The following year, my county captain, Clive Rice approached me about playing for his team, Transvaal. He was acting on a request from the administrators in Johannesburg. They were offering 15,000 rand, about £9,000. It was very tempting, but I couldn't afford the risk.

If I'd agreed, it had been quite clearly stated that I would jeopardise my Test status and my whole future outside cricket. My position in New Zealand enables me to reap financial benefit from a number of sources. The companies for whom I work may pull out because they'd feel they were indirectly supporting the South African regime.

In the short term it would have been very useful to earn a lump sum for playing in a single wicket competition or whatever, but long term, I'd have been cutting off my nose to spite my face. I've always been loyal to New Zealand cricket and there are still many things in domestic and world cricket I want to achieve before I give myself a 'benefit'. It may well be that a world team will be sent to South Africa when I retire from Test cricket. That is the time to accept and take the money, not at the start or in the middle of your career.

I wouldn't have done what Graham Gooch did, not at that stage of his life. It was a personal decision and obviously the financial rewards were very attractive, especially as he could earn overseas funds that might be lightly taxed. From Geoff Boycott's or Dennis Amiss' point of view it was slightly different. They no doubt thought that their Test days were over or coming to an end, so they were probably right to go.

The same applies to John Lever, Derek Underwood and Alan Knott. Some of the younger ones like Gooch, Larkins, Les Taylor, Sidebottom, Willey and Emburey might be regretting it.

It seems very strange that these players should be blamed when they did nothing wrong. I disagree with the three year ban, though, to be fair, each of the 'rebels' knew there was a danger of it happening. The only reason it did happen is that the Test and County Cricket Board was held to ransom by the black nations, India, Pakistan, the West Indies and Sri Lanka. The threat was that if the Board didn't take action, they wouldn't tour England. That would have meant jeopardising the livelihoods of all professionals. With no distribution of Test Match receipts, the counties would have collapsed. Sacrificing the rebel players for the security of English cricket was all the Board could do.

Wouldn't it be nice to see the cricket authorities in England, New Zealand and Australia take the bull by the horns and stop bowing to governmental pressure, or giving in to blackmail? The New Zealand Rugby Union had the courage to stand up for what it believed in. Although our politicians opposed the Springbok tour, they didn't stop it. The New Zealand Cricket Board won't take a risk. Perhaps it is waiting for England to take the lead.

Little or nothing has befallen rugby players from New Zealand or England who've had contact with South Africa. How can there be one law for rugby and another for cricket? I wonder what would really happen if the way was opened for South Africa? Would the black Test Match countries carry out their threat to boycott the white ones? Somehow I doubt it. West Indian cricket survives on tours. Cricket is the only thing which binds the islands together. Their team is a full-time professional touring circus which is probably busier than any other national team. How could it afford to miss trips to England and Australia? There wouldn't be much future in limiting the opposition to India, Pakistan and Sri Lanka.

The trouble is that such decisions are out of cricket's hands. Governments make the rules and the administrators abide by them. However, it's very disappointing to see politicians exploiting sportsmen. Disappointing and hypocritical. Trade with South Africa continues as normal, diplomatic relations continue (although the South African Consulate in New Zealand was closed in August 1984), but poor old cricket has to stop. By preventing me and others from going to South Africa, they are taking away my livelihood. If they were consistent about it, I might have more faith in them.

I am very much against apartheid, but it is South Africa's problem, not mine. Whether or not I play cricket there isn't likely to change the system. The British athletes Sebastian Coe, Steve Ovett and Daley Thompson who defied Mrs Thatcher and went to the Moscow Olympics realised that. They weren't condoning the Soviet system by competing. All they wanted to do was to practice their art.

Look at the anomalies. It's alright for me to stay with a South African in England and play in the same county team. It's alright for Indians, Pakistanis and West Indies to play with and against South Africans in England. But when it comes to doing the same thing in South Africa, suddenly it's unacceptable.

During the 1983 World Cup in England, the West Indies Cricket Board refused to give their team permission to play against Yorkshire in a practice match because the Yorkshire side included Boycott and Sidebottom who'd been on the rebel tour to South Africa. Quite rightly, Yorkshire refused to withdraw the two players and the game was cancelled. Interestingly, Lancashire agreed to play the West Indies instead. Rain washed out what would have been a fascinating situation because the South African pace bowler, Steve Jeffries who played against Boycott and Sidebottom in that series, would have been in the Lancashire line-up!

Notice that the West Indies didn't object to Allan Lamb playing against them last season?

Another incident highlights the stupidity of it all. My Notts colleague, Mike Hendrick was one of the 'rebels' on the Gooch tour. Like the rest, he was banished from Test cricket for three years. In the middle of the ban, however, 'Hendo' was invited to play in one of those 'gin and tonic' exhibitions in the Middle East. Not much was heard about it, and I'm not surprised. The opposition was the Indian team which had just won the World Cup. There was Hendo playing against and socialising with the Indian Test side and no-one batted an eyelid!

The Zola Budd story amazes me too. Presumably because Britain likes the idea of another possible Olympic medal, the formalities are rushed through in double quick time for a South African athlete to become British almost overnight. She competes in Los Angeles along with dozens of black nations who raise no objection, then goes back to Bloemfontain to continue being a South African. If she does stay in South Africa, I think that's a little unfair. Zola or her family really ought to decide which nation she belongs to. You can't keep changing for the sake of expediency.

Early this year, my family and I spent a few days at Clive Rice's home in Johannesburg before beginning the English season. The idea was suggested by the New Zealand Cricket Board which was anxious to see me over my breakdown. I couldn't believe it. Anyway, I went and although I was only there for a short time, I saw a little of what South Africa has done to make sport multi-racial. There are still plenty of things which upset me but I was impressed at the strides they'd made.

My father was a member of the International Cricket Conference fact-finding mission to South Africa in 1979. The delegates all reported that they were satisfied that cricket was becoming genuinely multi-racial, and that teams were indeed being picked on merit. In short, all the ICC's criteria had been met. That was nearly six years ago and to this day, the ICC has refused to admit South Africa back into Test cricket. What more do the cricket authorities there have to do?

They've made sweeping changes. Since they can't alter government policies, surely ICC countries should accept South Africa on that basis.

All member countries of the Conference agree that selection of teams should be left entirely to the governing bodies of the countries concerned. It's not permissible for another country to try to influence the selection of a team, whether for political reasons or any other. And yet, the black nations were directly influencing the selection of England's team by refusing to tour if the 'rebels' weren't banned. England has been forced for three years to pick a sub-standard team because other nations have said so. That is absolutely contrary to the ICC code. The situation is full of inconsistencies. It seems to me that the Conference is trying to administer cricket in the best interests of everyone except South Africa.

In the fullness of time, I believe that the rebel cricket tours by Gooch's 'Dirty Dozen', by Sri Lanka, and by the West Indians will turn out to be beneficial to world cricket. Kerry Packer's World Series was seen as a threat to the establishment but now many of his ideas have been adopted and cricket has prospered.

Because of the ICC's stubborness, South Africa had no choice but to go through the back door and contract some of the world's leading players. They'd been deprived of international competition since 1970, and must have been shattered to be shut out again after complying with all the stipulations. I sympathise with them and agree with what they were trying to do. They believed they could compete against the best in the world and we all knew they were right. Even now, they could pick a team which would give the West Indians a run for their money.

Gooch's team was by no means England's strongest, but it was probably no weaker than Gower's current squad. They were outplayed by Rice's South Africans who won the three-match series 1-0 and defeated 'England' in all the one-day internationals.

Was that tour a negative one? Of course it wasn't. South African kids had their first chance to see the Springboks play international cricket. Multi-racial crowds were seen at all the matches and the rebels also played against mixed teams in order to promote multi-racial cricket.

The fact that Rice's team was all-white is co-incidental. He tells me that had there been an Indian or a coloured player good enough, he would have been picked. I've seen for myself that blacks and coloureds out there are more interested in soccer and rugby than cricket. They don't seem to share their West Indian brothers' love of the game.

The 'Dirty Dozen' broke the ice as far as international touring teams were concerned. Next to visit were Sri Lanka and they were heavily beaten in all three Tests and all five one-dayers. As a cricket tour it was pretty hopeless, but it did at least show that blacks can be treated as human beings in a society which is supposed to behave in exactly the opposite fashion.

Lawrence Rowe's West Indians broke down all the barriers by touring South Africa. They drew the series 1-1 and lost 3-2 in the one-day games. With players like Kallicharran, Collis King, Rowe, Sylvester Clarke and others, it was by no means a scratch outfit. The crowds showed their appreciation of that by flocking to the games and the West Indians became heroes in South Africa.

Odd isn't it that Alvin Kallicharran is a hero in South Africa, but completely ostracized by his homeland? The fact that he plays there is proof that he's helping to break down racial barriers. Obviously he makes good money out of it, but if things had been so unbearable for blacks, presumably he wouldn't have gone in the first place. Now he lives there because he's banned from the West Indies. He says his former team mates won't even talk to him.

Politics has nothing to do with sport. As a professional cricketer, I want to play with and against the best in the world. I'm sure I speak for all cricketers when I say it's a terrible shame that some of the best players in the world, Rice, Proctor, Graeme Pollock, Garth Le Roux, Vincent van der Bijl, Ken McEwan and others have hardly been seen on international cricket fields outside their own country. Sadly, it seems that situation will continue for many years unless one of the major white cricket nations decides to put an end to the hypocrisy once and for all.

15

Extras

To most of his fellow cricketers, Hadlee's an enigma. With the possible exception of Boycott, they won't have seen anyone as thoroughly absorbed in his game. The world outside might not exist!

He answers to 'Paddles'—a nickname given to him by a schoolmaster because of the size and angle of his feet. His old New Zealand colleague, Glenn Turner used to swear that you could tell the time of day by looking at Hadlee's feet. It was either ten to two or a quarter to three when he was tired.

My superstitions are 111,222 and facing a hat-trick. I love roast lamb and listening to John Denver music. Peter Sellers' 'Pink Panther' movies are my favourites, but in general, I enjoy action movies most of all. I like electronic equipment and, when we win, I enjoy a cigar. I like to be well organised and hate being interrupted when I'm busy.

So there! Ken Taylor would certainly hesitate before interrupting Hadlee's train of thought.
'I probably don't ask his opinion as much as I should, but he's usually so wrapped up in what he's doing that you don't feel you want to intrude. Richard definitely lives on his nerves and is eager to get on with the job in hand. You won't find him wasting time. Cricketers and cricket followers are great ones for putting their feet up with a pint in their hands and philosophising about everything under the sun. Not Richard. He'll rarely talk about anything but cricket, and only

objectively about that. I suppose you could say he's a loner, contented with his own company. He's a great listener though, with a very good sense of humour.'

That sense of humour has led Hadlee to keep a collection of funny stories and incidents in a folder at home. He's a compulsive collector. If he sees or hears anything off-beat on the cricket circuit, he'll jot it down during the idle hours in the dressing room, and file it away. Here is a sample of those stories, beginning with his most embarrassing moment.

It was at Lords in 1978. We were playing the Third Test against England. People who've seen me bowl will know that I cross my legs and perform a little skip before getting mobile on my run-up to the wicket. At the start of the innings, I'd just crossed my legs and begun to run in when I found I wasn't running at all. I'd tripped over my feet—not difficult—and landed flat on my face. Crowd and players alike thought it was a great joke. It was bad enough doing that in a Test match, but at the home of cricket in front of 28,000 spectators and millions more on television . . .

Almost as embarrasing was when a young autograph hunter brought me crashing down to earth. I was making my debut for Canterbury in 1971, having come in as a replacement for my brother, Dayle. The autograph hunters beseiged us at the end of the game and one little lad asked me to sign. In his book I could see the names of several Test players and felt honoured to be in such company. When I'd signed, the boy looked up and asked:

'Who the hell are you?'

I said I was Richard Hadlee, a new player.

'Oh!' he replied, 'that's a nuisance, I don't want your autograph, how can I rub it out?'

There are many stories about Derek Randall, inevitably because he's the joker in the pack. Sometimes his humour's intentional, sometimes accidental. He has an unfortunate history of being involved in run-outs. More often than not, his partner is the one who suffers. Playing at Lords a season or two back, Derek was in fine form, hitting the ball to all parts of the boundary. He raced away to 80, but ran three of his team mates out in the process! In the dressing room, we waited for 'Arkle' to return to give him a bit of a blast. He arrived back and before we could get a word out, he spiked our guns with:

'Sorry fellas, I've been batting like Wally Hammond, but calling like Charlie Chaplin.'

In the 1982 Test series against India, Derek was recalled to the England side after a four-year absence. In the First Test at Lords, he scored a magnificent 120-odd. At the end of the day he was very tired and returned immediately to his hotel to rest up. Arriving back at his room, he tried to open the door with his key, but couldn't. This lasted for a minute or two, at the end of which, Derek was starting to get very irritated. He decided to complain to the manager.

'This bloody door won't open,' he said.

'I'm not at all surprised, sir,' came the reply, 'you're in the wrong hotel.'

Most cricketers who tour India and Pakistan suffer from stomach troubles of one sort or another. Derek was no exception. In between matches, he was on the golf course ready to tee off when he had to disappear rather sharpish behind some bushes. He called from beyond the undergrowth:

'Has anyone got any toilet paper?'

'No,' was the answer, 'but for goodness sake hurry up, there are people waiting to tee off after us.'

'Anyone got any newspaper then?'

Again the reply was 'No'.

Finally, in desperation: 'What about change for a ten quid note?'

While New Zealand were in India, one of the players, Robert Anderson was suffering badly from diarrhoea. He asked David O'Sullivan, who was as fit as a fiddle, how to cure the 'runs'. Daffy replied: 'If nothing else works, try Bisto.'

'Will that get rid of them?' Jumbo inquired hopefully.

'No,' said Daffy, 'but it'll sure thicken them up!'

Ian Botham was one of several nominations for the English 'Sportsman of the Year' a few years back. Seb Coe eventually took the award and Botham, who was on a tour of India sent

144

Coe a congratulatory telegram. It read: 'Congratulations on your award. Well deserved. I bet I could beat you in a race to the toilet. My run would be wind-assisted!'

Some of the hotel service in India was less than we're used to. In Hyderabad, we stayed in a low-ranked hotel . . . probably minus five stars! 'Jumbo' was fed up with the poor selection of food and asked the waiter for six boiled eggs for breakfast. Each egg had to be boiled for five minutes. 'Jumbo' wasn't the most diplomatic of travellers. He told the waiter in no uncertain terms:

'If those eggs aren't here in two minutes, I'll hang you on the coat peg! (or words to that effect).

Australia presents different problems. A town called Wagga Wagga is the home of flies. When we played there during the 1980-81 tour, our bowlers and fielders were reluctant to appeal for anything. Jeremy Coney came up with the answer:

'If you're brave enough to appeal, lads, make sure your teeth are together!' We all became ventriloquists that match.

On the 1982-83 tour of Australia and New Zealand, the English wicket-keeper, Ian Gould was having a disastrous match in the third one-day international at Lancaster Park, Christchurch. He dropped Bruce Edgar early in the innings and then was out for 0. Back in the pavilion, he was asked: 'Do you think Bob Taylor would have done better today?'

Gould replied:

'Never mind about Bob Taylor, ELIZABETH Taylor could have done better than that!'

Derek Randall has always said he'd love to captain Notts and he got his chance against Surrey in a Natwest game at Trent Bridge. Rice left the field for a couple of overs to change his boots — that was the official version anyhow. The skipper had bowled half of his twelve-over allocation. At that time, there was no vice-captain and Rice had shot off in such a hurry that he didn't leave any instructions. The umpires looked at me for guidance. I said: 'Sorry, it's nothing to do with me.' Basher Hassan didn't want the job, and John Birch, the youngest pro wasn't keen on taking the responsibility either. We all turned to Arkle. No-one in their right mind would give him the job because he doesn't usually keep track of the play. Nevertheless, he accepted the challenge.

He had to make an immediate decision—who would bowl while Rice was off the field? He looked at the scoreboard to assess the situation. There was a long delay. Finally, Derek asked Kevin Saxelby to bowl. Nineteen runs came from the over! At the end of the day, we asked Derek about his decision. This is what he said:

'My mind went completely blank when I looked at the scoreboard. I couldn't even read it and my legs started to buckle. I panicked and wished like hell that Rice would return. I couldn't even set a field for poor old Sax.'

For the record, we lost—by 20 runs!

One of the funniest things I saw on a cricket field was at Trent Bridge when Notts were playing Yorkshire in a Sunday League match in 1981. Pete Hacker had opened the bowling and 20 runs came from four overs. The small Yorkshire contingent around the boundary gave him a hard time with a few choice insults. Hacker was taken off and sent to deep mid-off when our left arm spinner, Noddy Bore came into the attack.

Graham Stevenson, one of the hardest-hitting batsmen, lofted a steepling catch to Hacker and he stood under the ball, watching all the way before taking the catch. He turned to the Yorkshire contingent, raising the ball to them in one hand then the other. The crowd loved it and beckoned him over to the boundary. In the meantime, Stevenson and Bairstow were on their third run, because the umpire had called 'no ball'. The two batsmen were nearly falling over themselves with mirth and Derek Randall was helpless with his feet in the air. I had to run over to Hacker and tell him in no uncertain terms to 'throw the bloody thing back.' Our captain, Clive Rice and poor old Noddy weren't amused.

Talking of Noddy Bore, he invented a wonderful device during a Benson and Hedges match against Warwickshire a couple of seasons back. Bob Willis was bowling pretty fast and short and Noddy, our number eleven wasn't too impressed. As he sat quaking, waiting to bat, he hit upon an idea. Getting hold of his helmet, he somehow attached a white handkerchief which rested on the lid. The would-be

146

flag was attached to a piece of string. In the case of a short-pitched ball, a quick tug of the string would raise the handkerchief and signal his surrender. Luckily for him, he didn't have to bat that day — but he's keeping the contraption just in case!

Going back a few years, I heard the story of Colin Milburn, the former Northants and England batsman who was trying his comeback at Derby one day. Milburn, sadly, lost an eye in a car accident, but was managing to bowl his gentle seamers from the scoreboard end. All of a sudden, he yelled: 'Stop the game, my glass eye has fallen out!' The players gathered around to look for the vital piece of equipment. Ollie eventually found it, licked it clean, and shoved it back in. The guys in the Derby dressing room thought it was a great joke. Someone asked what would have happened if he'd put it in back-to-front?

'That's easy,' said Mike Hendrick, 'he'd have to bowl from the other end!'

Most cricketers have a store of excuses for their mistakes. 'It kept low' or 'It did a bit' usually mean the batsman missed a straight one! Eddie Hemmings, my Notts colleague usually fields wearing glasses. On this particular occasion, he didn't. He dropped one comfortable catch then called for the twelfth man to bring out his specs. Within a few minutes, Eddie had fumbled another one to the ground, whereupon he stood with his hands on his hips and said:

'Bloody twelfth man — only brought out my reading glasses didn't he?'

Coming back to my old pal, Derek Randall. I remember he was having a lean period with the bat when we went to play Sussex at Hove. It was a greentop and Imran was at his fiery best. Derek was bowled first ball and walked back thoroughly disgruntled to the pavilion. As he passed Clive he quipped: 'It's all your bloody fault. Fancy sending me out in the middle of a hat-trick!'

Although 210 is my highest score, the local newspaper in Nottingham once had me breaking every record in sight. A supporter noticed this scoreboard:

NOTTINGHAM v LANCASHIRE at TRENT BRIDGE

Nottingham

P. Todd	c Wallwork b Folley	3
T. Robinson	c Lloyd (D) b Allott	26
D. Randall	c Reidy b Croft	21
C. Rice	c Wallwork b Reidy	31
M. Fell	b Lloyd (D)	26
R. Hadlee	not out	3821
B. French	b Croft	2
E. Hemmings	not out	0
	Extras	12
	Total (6 wickets)	**159**

The letter also said: 'Your magnificent knock makes Graham Gooch's 198 in a one-day game look small beer!' For the record I scored 70—work that one out!

I loved the advert Notts cricket manager, Ken Taylor put up for a new secretary after his previous one, Julie had emigrated to Australia. Ken, who's in his mid-sixties, worded it this way:

Nottinghamshire County Cricket Club
Secretary (female)

Required for the cricket manager. Shorthand would be bloody marvellous, but not absolutely essential. Unsociable hours but many fringe benefits and attractive setting. Applicants must be capable of using initiative but will not be required to pick the team (not to begin with anyway). Salary negotiable according to age and experience. The successful applicant must be sexually attractive but is not permitted to pinch the manager's bottom! Please apply in writing.

Believe it or not, he received 150 applications!

My Kiwi teammates call me 'Superman' because I've produced the occasional matchwinning performance. In 1980, I was awarded the trophy for 'New Zealand Sportsman of the Year'. We were on tour in Australia at the time. When we arrived in Newcastle for a three-day game, a bouquet of flowers was delivered to me at the ground. I thought there

148

must be some mistake. Who'd send a New Zealander flowers, least of all me? The card read: 'Congratulations on the award from Lois Lane and the staff at the *Daily Planet*'! Stephen Boock was apparently the instigator.

Not all my letters and messages are complimentary. The following one came to the team hotel in Colombo during the Sri Lanka tour. It was after the Third Test. Earlier, Wettimuny, the Sri Lankan batsman had been hit in the box by one of my deliveries and in the last Test, Ranjan Madugalle failed to avoid a bouncer and took a blow on the head. Both players had to leave the field and by the time they returned, the games were beyond recall. The letter was sent to 'Greig Howarth, captain' and marked 'for the attention of John Hadlee'!

Dear Sir,

It is with great reluctance that as a Sri Lankan lover of this honourable game is writing this note to your good self.

The performance of your Hadlee is rather degrading. You would have noticed what he did to break up the partnership in the Second Test between our Sidath Wetthamuny and Roy Dias.

He did the same to our Ranjan Madugalla in the Thired Test by injuring him when the pratnership was on with Arjuna, Ranathunga and Madugalla.

This sort of low tactics is done by the uneducated people and not by the educated as you all. The game should be played on its merits. Just because your Hadlee could not get him out he had adopted his third grade low method by injuring the players.

This itself shows that your Hadlee is not a SPORTSMAN who is fit to play for your country and for your team under your management. It is a disgrace to have a person of this calibur in your honourable side to represent New Zealend.

Please tell him with our compliments that he is a THIRD RATE SELFISH UNSPORTY . . .

Keep this phrase in mind,

Throughly Dishartened Crickter,
Sri Lankan

In a similar vein, a cricket watcher from Newton Abbot in Devon sent me these words:

'Some people think you play good cricket. Well my idea of playing cricket doesn't mean bowling bouncers like you do. You are out to INJURE our men with those dreadful bouncers. In your first match against England you BADLY injured Chris Tavare. You could have broken his jaw. Had I been the umpire you would have been sent off . . . You think yourself high and mighty but you may get one before you finish . . . '

Somehow I don't think he liked me! I don't get too many like that fortunately. Perhaps if the chap had signed his name it would have meant more. There was no point trying to reason with people like that. They want the best of both worlds. It's alright for Bob Willis to bounce our batsmen, but we aren't allowed to bounce back.

The following letter is one of my proudest possessions, even though it is rather amusing: This is how it came:

NEWJILAND.
TO RICHARD HEDALY
WORLD FAMOUS PLAYER OF CRICKET
NEWJILAND.

It was from:

SUMON SONI
SON OF MR. JAI KISHAN SONI
BATHARIYON KA CHOWK
NAGPUR 341001
INDIA

The letter.

Jai

Bathariyon Ka Chowk,
Nagpur.
29th June 1982

Dear Richard Hedaly,
I am your fan. I am very interested in your records. Congratulation to you for meny world record.

150

Please introduce me them "Test Match", you think all-best. And please I want your autographed photo. Please send me your nice a photo.

I am sorry that I don't know your address. Plese answered my letter sure and send me your photo.

I wait your letter,
Your praiser,
Suman Soni.

An avid fan by the name of Iris Timmings from New Zealand regularly sends me poems. As you can see, she has quite a talent. She's typical of thousands of housewives back home who get involved in cricket. Many a New Zealand husband has had to go without his dinner when cricket's on the television. This was a tribute to our historic victory over England at Headingley in 1983.

HOWZAT!

You're magnificent, splendid — superb
You've made us so proud, we're euphoric
Geoff and team you have conquered those Poms
In a victory that's truly historic.

You're tops in the sporting tradition
Our small country incredibly breeds
With that glorious test win — first ever
There in England, at Headingley, Leeds.

Jubilation abounds round this country
For each Pakeha, Islander, Maori
We're dancing the hula and haka
In Christchurch and Waipapakauri!

To field first, said the BBC gents,
Was tempting an unhappy fate.
Geoff proved he knows what he's doing
And has his head on very straight.

And you guys gave Taylor the stitch
And poor Fowler you plucked like a turkey
And Botham you handled with ease
So his future now looks very murky.

151

When Lamb gave our bowlers a roasting
Pommie bleating was starting to grow
But Cairns' bowling had that Lamb chopping
And unsheepishly taken by Crowe.

Our Lance didn't dally with Dilley
Gave Randall a mighty surprise
And the ball he cooked up for poor Edmonds
Was one that was 'sure to rise'.

And then when their total was growing
And old chums — life was no cabaret
Still hungry and lean came on Coney
And quickly drummed out Tavare.

What a prince was our Edgar the Bruce
We mourned as he limping, departed
Like his namesake of old — tried again
And finished, so well, what he'd started.

The Smithy, so says the old poem,
Had arms that were like iron bands
Every catch it was firmly imprisoned
In our Smithy's safe steely hands.

He's fire, he's ice and he's tempest
Our all-rounder — the finest you'll see
He's Mars, he's Apollo, he's Atlas
He's all talent — he's Richard Hadlee!

And during the Pommies last innings
Didn't Chatfield just make wickets fly
Line and length he nagged and succeeded
Back at Lords there was not a dry eye!

And John Wright — a warrior, battler
He crafted that brave ninety-three
Every man played his part in the build-up
On the way to this great victory.

And rampaging that last hour was Willis
Who gave a faint chance you may buckle
We can't put our feelings on paper —
For we've bitten our nails to the knuckle.

Revenge it was sweet — it was justice
For our teams of the last fifty years

152

For the patronisation we've suffered
And the spilling of blood, sweat and tears.

Now we're living it up, here down under
Champagne by the magnum we gargle
We're delighted, delirious, gloating
From North Cape to deep south Invercargill.

And when you return to New Zealand
Grand receptions and parties you'll grace
If you ever come over to Gisborne—
There'll be tea and hot scones at my place.

So, knights of the leather and willow
Take up your armour and swords
Up there and at 'em—we're with you
And good luck for the next one at Lords!

Iris Timmings

With early autumn just beginning to edge the leaves with brown, Hadlee, Karen and young Nicholas packed their bags again for home. It had been an outstanding season, and Hadlee knew he'd be going back to a royal welcome down under. The family took the slow route home, via Disneyland, Waikiki beach, Honolulu and Fiji. You could say he'd earned a break. Before reaching Christchurch and his five-acre small holding, there was one more surprise in store.

During their six-day holiday in Fiji, the family took a one-hour launch trip to Beachcomber Island, which barely merits a dot on the smallest of maps. In five minutes, you can complete a circular tour! To his amazement, there sunning himself was Dennis Lillee!

It was marvellous to renew our association. We had a bit of a conversation and he congratulated me on reaching the double. I was a little surprised how much he knew about it. When you talk of it being a small world, there aren't many smaller places than Beachcomber Island to bump into one of your idols!

By early October, Hadlee was back in his natural habitat, pottering around the grounds of his lovely home

153

in Christchurch, 'dagging' and 'drenching' sheep on the farm and tossing another steak onto the barbecue. He was struck by the extraordinarily high cost of living in Britain compared with New Zealand. It annoys him when he has to buy New Zealand lamb in England at three times the original cost back home. For the price of a roast leg of lamb (£5), he can buy an entire sheep in New Zealand!

We have to buy relatively cheap meats in Nottingham because of the expense. Things like sausages and mince are quite common, whereas in New Zealand we'd indulge in a roast meal every day. Every day that is, except Friday which is traditionally fish and chip night back home. If you think English fish and chips are good, you should taste the ones we make in New Zealand!

Hadlee will be back in England for two more summers, injury permitting. After the New Zealand tour in 1986, he will probably call it a day. Until he does, he still has unfinished business:

I shall try to achieve the double all over again next season, and will plan it in exactly the same way. It'll be very hard to better my performance, but if the weather's kind again; if I stay clear of injury; if I get the batting opportunities, and if the other guys hold catches for me, it's possible. Injury is the key, I'm not basically strong enough physically to push myself through this amount of work indefinitely.

Apart from that, I badly want to win something again with Notts. We made a Lords final in 1982 and crashed out disgracefully so that's one ambition. Whether it's the Natwest or the Benson and Hedges I want to go back to Lords to set the record straight. It was annoying to finish runners-up in the John Player League as well as the championship. I wouldn't mind that title as well. We won more away games than any other county in the Sunday League, but our efforts at Trent Bridge were diabolical. If we can sort that out, I'm convinced we have a great chance of going all the way next season.

Let's not forget the championship. Winning it once and coming so close a second time makes me want to win it again.

If Mike Hendrick's fit, it will make all the difference. There'll be pressure on Clive Rice. He'll only bowl out of necessity but he'll have plenty on his plate with the captaincy and his benefit year to sort out. I hope he doesn't overdo it. There were times last season when I thought I could sense the same thing happening to him that happened to me.

Finishing second in the championship, second in the Player League, semi-finalists in the Benson and Hedges made it our best overall season. Next season it's vital that we have success and win something. I want to be part of it.

As you can appreciate, I've become a statistical player. It may mean nothing to anyone else, but it's become my whole reason for playing cricket. The double was one mark along the way. Now I want the test double of 2,000 runs and 200 wickets. I need another 180 runs for that target. I'm also chasing 1,000 wickets in first-class cricket.

These are things that keep me turning up year after year. Until I achieve them I won't rest. Once I've done it all, perhaps I can sit back and say to myself: 'Right, no more targets, Paddles. Be happy with what you've done — now go and put your feet up!'

Shortly before flying back to New Zealand to chase another summer, Hadlee dropped into Trent Bridge to say his goodbyes. Ken Taylor congratulated him on a magnificent season; adding: 'You've proved yourself the greatest cricketer in Great Britain today.'

Hadlee's reply was typical:

'Thanks, Ken, that's something for me to live up to next season.'

1984 COUNTY SEASON – BATTING

Debut Notts 1978 – Cap – 1978

H.S. 1st Class. Previous Best 142* v Yorkshire at Bradford 1981
210* v Middlesex – Lords 1984

Date	Opponent	Venue	Match	Inns	N.O.	Runs	Total Runs	Avge	H.S.	C	S
April											
28-29-30	Surrey	Trent Bridge	1	1	-	11 c	11 c	11.00	11	1	-
28-29-30	Surrey	Trent Bridge				Did not bat				2/3	-
May											
2-3-4	Leicestershire	Trent Bridge	2	2	-	14 c	25	12.50	14	1/4	-
2-3-4	Leicestershire	Trent Bridge	2	3	1	25*	50	25.00	25*	-/4	-
9-10-11	Yorkshire	Headingley	3			Did not bat				-/4	-
9-10-11	Yorkshire	Headingley	3	4	1	1 b	51	17.00	25*	-/4	-
23-24-25	Essex	Chelmsford	4	5	2	71*	122	40.66	71*	2/6	-
23-24-25	Essex	Chelmsford	4			Did not bat					
26-28-29	Derbyshire	Derby	5			Did not bat				-/6	-
26-28-29	Derbyshire	Derby	5	6	3	10*	132	44.00	71*	-/6	-
May June											
30-31-1	Warwickshire	Edgbaston	6			Did not bat				1/7	-
June											
2-4-5	Hampshire	B'mouth	7	7	4	100*	232	77.33	100*	2/9	-
2-4-5	Hampshire	B'mouth	7	8	4	37 c	269	67.25	100*	1/10	-
9-11-12	Glamorgan	Trent Bridge	8	9	4	71 c	340	68.00	100*	1/11	-
9-11-12	Glamorgan	Trent Bridge	8			Did not bat				-/11	-
16-18-19	Gloucestershire	Trent Bridge	9	10	4	17 c	357	54.50	100*	-/11	-
16-18-19	Gloucestershire	Trent Bridge				Did not bat				-/11	-
23-25-26	Leicestershire	Leicester	10	11	4	9 c	366	52.28	100*	-/11	-
23-25-26	Leicestershire	Leicester	10			Did not bat				-/11	-
27-28-29	Yorkshire	Trent Bridge	11								

Date	Opponent	Venue				Score	Avg	HS	
7-9-10	Sussex	Trent Bridge	12	13	4	67 c 449	49.88	100*	-/15	-
11-12-13	Somerset	Trent Bridge	13	14	4	41 c 490	49.00	100*	-/15	-
11-12-13	Somerset	Trent Bridge	13	15	4	6 c 496	45.09	100*	-/15	-
14-16-17	Worcestershire	Trent Bridge	14	16	4	0 c 496	41.33	100*	2/17	-
14-16-17	Worcestershire	Trent Bridge	14			Did not bat			-/17	-
28-30-31	Lancashire	Trent Bridge	15	17	4	17 c 513	39.46	100*	-/17	-
28-30-31	Lancashire	Trent Bridge	15			Did not bat			-/17	-
Aug									
4-6-7	Worcestershire	Worcester	16	18	4	70 c 583	41.64	100*	1/18	-
4-6-7	Worcestershire	Worcester	16	19	5	21* 604	43.14	100*	-/18	-
8-9-10	Derbyshire	Trent Bridge	17	20	5	56 c 660	44.00	100*	-/18	-
8-9-10	Derbyshire	Trent Bridge	17	21	5	10 c 670	41.87	100*	-/18	-
11-13-14	Middlesex	Lords	18	22	6	210* 880	55.00	210*	1/19	-
18-20-21	Kent	Folkestone	19	23	6	51 c 931	54.76	210*	1/20	-
18-20-21	Kent	Folkestone	19	24	7	10* 941	55.35	210*	-/20	-
22-23-24	Lancashire	Blackpool	20	25	7	38 c 979	54.38	210*	-/20	-
22-23-24	Lancashire	Blackpool	20			Did not bat			1/21	-
25-27-28	Warwickshire	Trent Bridge	21	26	7	39 c 1018	53.57	210*	-/21	-
25-27-28	Warwickshire	Trent Bridge	21			Did not bat			-/21	-
29-30-31	Northamptonshire	Trent Bridge	22	27	7	78 c 1096	54.80	210*	-/21	-
29-30-31	Northamptonshire	Trent Bridge	22			Did not bat			-/21	-
Sept									
5-6-7	Sussex	Hove	23	28	7	31 c 1127	53.66	210*	1/22	-
5-6-7	Sussex	Hove	23	29	8	14* 1141	54.33	210*	-/22	-
8-10-11	Somerset	Taunton	24	30	8	10 c 1151	52.31	210*	1/23	-
8-10-11	Somerset	Taunton	24	31	8	28 c 1179	51.26	210*	-/23	-
			1 x 200	1 x 100	6 x 50				
Budget			20	33	-	1000	34.00	-	25	-
Total			24	31	-	1179	51.26	-	23	-

c = caught, b = bowled, * = not out

157

1984 COUNTY SEASON – BOWLING

BB 1st Class—
7-23 v India – N.Z. 1975-6
7-23 v Sussex – 1979 – Nottm.

Date	Opponent		Venue	Overs	T.O.	Mdn	TM	R	TR	W	TW	AV	W	NB
April														
28-29-30	Surrey	W	Trent Bridge	19.3	19.3	13	13	8	8	4	4	2.00	-	-
28-29-30	Surrey	W	Trent Bridge	8.1	27.4	3	16	14	22	4	8	2.75	-	-
May														
2-3-4	Leicestershire		Trent Bridge	24	51.4	6	22	68	90	2	10	9.00	-	1
2-3-4	Leicestershire		Trent Bridge	20	71.4	7	29	47	137	-	10	13.70	-	1/2
9-10-11	Yorkshire		Headingley	18.5	90.3	4	33	62	199	1	11	18.09	-	1/3
				Did not bowl								-	-	-/3
23-24-25	Essex	W	Chelmsford	13	103.3	4	37	32	231	1	12	19.25	-	-/3
23-24-25	Essex	W	Chelmsford	27	130.3	11	48	52	283	6	18	15.72	-	-/3
26-28-29	Derbyshire		Derby	24	154.3	9	57	40	323	2	20	16.15	-	-/3
26-28-29	Derbyshire		Derby	6	160.3	5	62	3	326	-	20	16.30	-	-/3
May June														
30-31-1	Warwickshire		Edgbaston	17	177.3	3	65	40	366	-	20	18.30	-	-/3
30-31-1	Warwickshire		Edgbaston	6	183.3	3	68	7	373	-	20	18.65	-	-/3
June														
2-4-5	Hampshire	W	B'mouth	26	209.3	10	78	51	424	2	22	19.27	-	-/3
2-4-5	Hampshire	W	B'mouth	18	227.3	7	85	35	459	5	27	17.00	-	-/3
9-11-12	Glamorgan		Trent Bridge	16	243.3	5	90	31	490	2	29	16.89	-	-/3
9-11-12	Glamorgan		Trent Bridge	12	255.3	5	95	25	518	2	31	16.70	-	-/3
16-18-19	Gloucester's	W	Trent Bridge	15.3	271	7	102	35	553	7	38	14.55	-	-/3
16-18-19	Gloucester's	W	Trent Bridge	18	289	4	106	41	594	4	42	14.14	-	-/3
23-25-26	Leicestershire		Leicester	27	316	7	113	60	654	3	45	14.53	-	-/3

Date	Opponent	Venue	O	Cum O	M	Cum M	R	Cum R	W	Cum W	Avge	5w	Best
7-9-10	Sussex	Trent Bridge	10	379	5	135	6	789	4	57	13.84	-	-/3
11-12-13	Somerset	Trent Bridge	22	401	7	142	45	834	4	61	13.67	-	-/3
11-12-13	Somerset	Trent Bridge	12	413	3	145	31	865	2	63	13.73	-	-/3
14-16-17	Worcestershire	Trent Bridge	13	426	4	149	22	887	1	64	13.85	-	-/3
14-16-7	Worcestershire	Trent Bridge	18	444	2	151	61	948	5	69	13.73	-	-/3
28-30-31	Lancashire	Trent Bridge	19.2	463.2	6	157	49	997	4	73	13.65	-	3/6
28-30-31	Lancashire	Trent Bridge	23	486.2	6	163	48	1045	2	75	13.93	-	1/7
Aug													
4-6-7	Worcestershire	Worcester	23	509.2	11	174	41	1086	1	76	14.28	-	1/8
8-9-10	Derbyshire	Trent Bridge	13	522.2	1	175	30	1116	4	80	13.95	-	-/8
8-9-10	Derbyshire	Trent Bridge	25	547.2	9	184	47	1163	3	83	14.01	-	-/8
11-13-14	Middlesex W	Lords	20	567.2	4	188	55	1218	4	87	14.00	-	-/8
11-13-14	Middlesex W	Lords	10	577.2	2	190	14	1232	1	88	14.00	-	-/8
18-20-21	Kent	Folkestone	28	605.2	9	199	51	1283	3	91	14.09	-	1/9
18-20-21	Kent	Folkestone	20	625.2	6	205	49	1332	2	93	14.32	-	1/10
22-23-24	Lancashire W	Blackpool	14	639.2	2	207	32	1364	2	95	14.35	-	3/13
22-23-24	Lancashire W	Blackpool	18.4	658.0	6	213	40	1404	5	100	14.04	-	-/13
25-27-28	Warwickshire W	Trent Bridge	26.2	684.2	9	222	55	1459	6	106	13.76	-	-/13
25-27-28	Warwickshire W	Trent Bridge	24	708.2	7	229	48	1507	3	109	13.82	1	-/13
29-30-31	Northamptonshire	Trent Bridge	13	721.2	3	232	26	1533	3	112	13.68	-/1	-/13
					Did not bowl								
Sept													
5-6-7	Sussex	Hove	23	744.2	7	239	40	1573	1	113	13.92	-	2/15
					Did not bowl								
8-10-11	Somerset	Taunton	23	767.2	8	247	59	1632	4	117	13.94	-	2/17
8-10-11	Somerset	Taunton	5	772.3	1	248	13	1645	1	117	14.05	1	-/17
	Budget			750		250		1500		100	15.00	-	-
	Total			772		248		1645		117	14.05		

1984 JOHN PLAYER LEAGUE

BOWLING

Date	Opponent		Venue	Overs	T.O.	Mdn	TM	R	TR	W	TW	AV	W	NB
May														
6	Essex		Chelmsford	8	8	-	-	37	37	2	2	18.5	1	-
13	Worcestershire		Worcester	8	16	1	-	42	79	-	2	39.5	-/1	-
20	Yorkshire		Hull	7	23	1	1	16	95	1	3	31.66	-	-
27	Derbyshire		Trent Bridge			Did not bowl								
June														
3	Hampshire	W	S'ton	8	31	2	3	32	127	1	4	31.75	-/1	-
10	Glamorgan		Trent Bridge	7	38	-	3	27	154	1	5	30.80	-/1	1
17	Gloucestershire		Trent Bridge	8	46	1	4	24	178	1	6	29.66	-/1	1/2
24	Leicestershire		Leicester	8	54	1	5	28	206	2	8	25.75	1/2	1/2
July														
5	Sussex	W	Trent Bridge	8	62	-	5	28	234	2	10	23.40	1/3	1/2
22	Northants		Trent Bridge	8	70	-	5	53	284	1	11	25.81	1/4	-/2
29	Lancashire		Trent Bridge	8	78	1	6	33	317	-	11	28.81	1/5	2/4
August														
12	Middlesex	W	Lords	8	86	1	7	31	348	1	12	29.00	-/5	-/4
19	Kent		Folkestone	8	94	1	8	20	365	4	16	23.00	-/5	1/5
26	Warwickshire		Trent Bridge	8	102	1	9	34	402	2	18	22.33	-/5	-/5
Sept														
3	Surrey	W	Trent Bridge	5	107	-	9	14	416	1	19	21.80	-/5	-/5
10	Somerset		Taunton	6	113	1	10	10	426	2	21	20.03	-/5	-/5

BATTING

Date	Opponent	Venue	Match	Inns	NO	Runs	Total Runs	Avge	HS	C	S
May											
6	Essex	Chelmsford	1	1	1	32 *	32	-	32*		
13	Worcestershire	Worcester	2			Did not bat					
20	Yorkshire	Hull	3	2	1	19 c	51	51.00	32*	-	-
27	Derbyshire	Trent Bridge	4			Did not bat					
June											
3	Hampshire	S'ton	5	3	1	35 c	86	43.00	35	1/1	
10	Glamorgan	Trent Bridge	6	4	1	12 c	98	32.66	-	1/2	
17	Gloucestershire	Trent Bridge	7	5	1	13 lbw	111	27.75	35	-/2	
24	Leicestershire	Leicester	8	6	2	32 *	143	35.75	35	1/3	
July											
8	Sussex	Trent Bridge	9	7	3	25 *	168	42.00	35	2/5	
22	Northants	Trent Bridge	10	8	3	47 b	215	43.00	47	1/6	
29	Lancashire	Trent Bridge	11	9	4	8 *	223	44.60	47	1/7	
Aug											
12	Middlesex	Lords	12	10	5	75 *	298	59.60	75*	1/8	
19	Kent	Folkestone	13	11	5	8 b	306	51.00	75*	-/8	
26	Warwickshire	Trent Bridge	14	12	5	21 ro	327	46.71	75*	-/8	
Sept											
3	Surrey	Trent Bridge	15	13	5	58 ro	385	48.00	75*	-/8	
10	Somerset	Taunton	16	14	5	14 c	399	44.30	75*	-/8	
	(Budget)	Games	10	10	-	-	250	25.0	-	-	-

ro = run out   c = caught
b = bowled   * = not out

16

Career Record

R. J. HADLEE
Test Career Record up to September 1984
Batting

	M	I	NO	Runs	HS	Avge	100s
1972-73 v Pakistan in New Zealand	1	1	0	46	46	46.00	0
1973-74 v England in England	1	2	1	4	4*	4.00	0
1973-74 v Australia in Australia	3	6	0	68	20	11.33	0
1973-74 v Australia in New Zealand	2	3	0	37	23	12.33	0
1975-76 v India in New Zealand	2	2	0	45	33	22.50	0
1976-77 v Pakistan in Pakistan	3	6	2	214	87	53.50	0
1976-77 v India in India	3	6	0	60	21	10.00	0
1976-77 v Australia in New Zealand	2	4	0	143	81	35.75	0
1977-78 v England in New Zealand	3	6	1	80	39	16.00	0
1978 v England in England	3	6	0	32	11	5.33	0
1978-79 v Pakistan in New Zealand	3	5	1	115	53*	28.75	0
1979-80 v West Indies in New Zealand	3	4	0	178	103	44.50	1
1980-81 v Australia in Australia	3	6	2	98	51*	24.50	0
1980-81 v India in New Zealand	3	4	0	29	20	7.25	0
1981-82 v Australia in New Zealand	3	5	1	92	40	23.00	0
1982-83 v Sri Lanka in New Zealand	2	3	1	59	30	29.50	0
1983 v England in England	4	8	2	301	92*	50.16	0
1983-84 v England in New Zealand	3	4	0	144	99	36.00	0
1983-84 v Sri Lanka in Sri Lanka	3	4	0	75	29	18.75	0
Total	50	85	11	1820	103	24.59	1

Notes

His highest innings was 103 v West Indies at Christchurch on February 24, 1980. He batted 1
minutes, hitting 2 sixes and 11 fours. He hit 99 v England at Christchurch on February 3, 198
batting 111 minutes with 18 fours. Combined with match bowling figures of 8 for 44, he was large
instrumental in bringing New Zealand victory by an innings and 132 runs.

R. J. HADLEE
Test Career Record up to September 1984
Bowling

	Overs	Mdns	Runs	Wkts	Avge	BB	5i	10m
972/73 v Pakistan in New Zealand	25	0	112	2	56.00	2-84	0	0
973 v England in England	45	8	143	1	143.00	1-79	0	0
973/74 v Australia in Australia	61.7	9	255	7	36.43	4-33	0	0
973/74 v Australia in New Zealand	52	6	225	10	22.90	4-75	0	0
975/76 v India in New Zealand	48.3	4	197	12	16.41	7-23	1	1
976/77 v Pakistan in Pakistan	75.2	2	447	10	44.70	5-121	1	0
976/77 v India in India	127	18	437	13	33.61	4-95	0	0
976/77 v Australia in New Zealand	72	7	354	6	59.00	3-133	0	0
977/78 v England in New Zealand	121.3	26	371	15	24.73	6-26	1	1
978 v England in England	121.1	31	270	13	20.76	5-85	1	0
978/79 v Pakistan in New Zealand	117.6	13	414	18	23.00	5-62	2	0
979/80 v West Indies in New Zealand	161.3	50	361	19	19.00	6-68	2	1
980/81 v Australia in Australia	147.3	35	364	19	19.15	6-57	2	0
980/81 v India in New Zealand	108.3	36	288	10	28.80	5-47	1	0
981/82 v Australia in New Zealand	91.5	25	226	14	16.14	6-100	2	0
982/83 v Sri Lanka in New Zealand	77.3	27	141	10	14.10	4-33	0	0
983 v England in England	232	65	559	21	26.61	6-53	2	0
983/84 v England in New Zealand	109.5	33	232	12	19.33	5-28	1	0
983/84 v Sri Lanka in Sri Lanka	117.5	47	230	23	10.00	5-29	2	1
Total 8 ball overs	579.2	59	5626	235	23.94	7-23	18	4
6 ball overs	1333.4	383						

otes

is best bowling in an innings was 7 for 23 in 8.3 overs v India at Wellington on February 17, 76. This fine analysis enabled New Zealand to dismiss India for 81 and win the Test by an innings d 33 runs. When he dismissed Norman Cowans in the 4th Test v England at Trent Bridge on ugust 28, 1983, Hadlee brought his total of Test wickets to 200—the first New Zealander to reach is figure; he had become the bowler to take most Test wickets for New Zealand in 1980, when ring the 1st Test v West Indies at Dunedin on February 13, he overtook the previous record of 6 wickets by Richard Collinge. Hadlee's eleven wickets for 102 in this game enabled New Zealand win by one wicket.

denotes 8-ball overs.

Career Record for Nottinghamshire
First Class Batting Averages

	M	I	NO	Runs	HS	Avge	100s	C
1978	7	8	4	193	101*	48.25	1	
1979	12	16	4	193	41	16.08	0	
1980	8	9	1	231	68	28.87	0	
1981	21	26	3	745	142*	32.39	1	
1982	18	28	2	807	131	31.04	2	
1983	5	4	0	119	103	29.75	1	
1984	24	31	8	1179	210*	51.26	2	2
Total	95	122	22	3467	210*	34.67	7	

Centuries

101* v Derbyshire (Trent Bridge)	1978
142* v Yorkshire (Bradford)	1981
131 v Surrey (Oval)	1982
100* v Worcestershire (Worcester)	1982
103 v Sussex (Hove)	1983
100* v Hampshire (Bournemouth)	1984
210* v Middlesex (Lords)	1984

His highest innings of 210* was hit in 356 minutes off 261 balls, with one six and twenty-fo
fours. It is the highest innings made for Notts at Lords since 1892, when A. Shrewsbury score
212. Hadlee's innings is the highest ever made for a Notts batsman coming in as low as No.

First Class Bowling Averages

	Overs	Mdns	Runs	Wkts	Avge	BB	5i	10
1978	216.3	48	555	37	15.00	6-39	4	
1979	317	103	753	47	16.02	7-23	2	
1980	222.1	82	410	29	14.13	5-32	1	
1981	708.4	231	1564	105	14.89	7-25	4	
1982	403.5	123	889	61	14.57	7-25	4	
1983	86.2	28	210	13	16.15	5-72	1	
1984	772.2	248	1645	117	14.06	7-35	6	
Total	2726.5	863	6026	409	14.73	7-23	22	

Notes

No other Notts bowler this century has taken 400 or more wickets for the County at such a lov
cost as Hadlee's 14.73 runs per wicket and in the whole history of Notts cricket his record i
beaten only by A. Shaw (898 wkts, av 11.52) and F. Morley (666, 12.26).

His best bowling in an innings for Notts is curiously the same as his best Test analysis, seve
for twenty-three. His Notts figures were against Sussex at Trent Bridge on July 3, 1979.

The Double
2,000 runs and 200 wickets in a season

G. H. Hirst   1906   2,385 runs and 208 wickets
                                 (including 111 and 117 not out and
                                 6-70 and 5-45 in one match for
                                 Yorkshire v Somerset at Bath).

3,000 runs and 100 wickets

J. H. Parks   1937   3,003 runs and 101 wickets

2,000 runs and 100 wickets

W. G. Grace	1873	2,139 runs and 106 wickets	
W. G. Grace	1876	2,622	129
C. L. Townsend	1899	2,440	101
G. L. Jessop	1900	2,210	104
G. H. Hirst	1904	2,501	132
G. H. Hirst	1905	2,266	110
W. Rhodes	1909	2,094	141
W. Rhodes	1911	2,261	117
F. A. Tarrant	1911	2,030	111
J. W. Hearne	1913	2,036	124
J. W. Hearne	1914	2,116	123
F. E. Woolley	1914	2,272	125
J. W. Hearne	1920	2,148	142
V. W. C. Jupp	1931	2,169	121
F. E. Woolley	1921	2,101	167
F. E. Woolley	1922	2,022	163
F. E. Woolley	1923	2,091	101
L. F. Townsend	1933	2,268	100
D. E. Davies	1937	2,012	103
James Langridge	1937	2,082	101
T. E. Bailey	1959	2,011	100

1,000 runs and 200 wickets

A. E. Trott	1899	1,175	239
A. E. Trott	1900	1,337	211
A. S. Kennedy	1922	1,129	205
M. W. Tate	1923	1,168	219
M. W. Tate	1924	1,419	205
M. W. Tate	1925	1,290	228

1,000 runs and 100 wickets

16 times	W. Rhodes
14	G. H. Hirst
10	V. W. C. Jupp
9	W. E. Astill
8	T. E. Bailey, W. G. Grace, M. S. Nichols, A. E. Rel F. A. Tarrant, M. W. Tate, F. J. Titmus, F. E. Woolley
7	G. E. Tribe
6	P. G. H. Fender, R. Illingworth, James Langridge
5	J. W. H. T. Douglas, J. W. Hearne, A. S. Kennedy, Newman
4	E. G. Arnold, J. Gunn, R. Kilner, B. R. Knight
3	W. W. Armstrong, L. C. Braund, G. Giffen, N. E. Haig, R. Howarth, C. B. Llewellyn, J. B. Mortimer, Ray Smith, S. G. Smith, L. F. Townsend, A. W. Wellard

Since the reduction of championship matches in 1969, only Richard Hadlee (1984) has achiev the double, with 1179 runs and 117 wickets. Fred Titmus had been the last to reach it 17 ye: earlier, in 1967. Only five players have scored 1,000 runs and taken seventy-five wickets (a mc realistic target these days). They are: Mushtaq Mohammad (1969), Tony Greig (1971), Richa Hutton (1971), Keith Boyce (1972) and Mike Proctor (1979).